Creating an Inclusive Worship Community

Accommodating All People at God's Table

A Parish Resource Book

Elizabeth Browne, Ph.D.

Liguori
LIGUORI, MISSOURI

Published by Liguori Publications
Liguori, Missouri
www.liguori.org
www.catholicbooksonline.com

Imprimi Potest:
Richard Thibodeau, C.Ss.R.
Provincial, Denver Province
The Redemptorists

Copyright 2004 by Elizabeth Browne
Library of Congress Catalog Control Number: 2003114729
ISBN 0-7648-1108-8

Printed in the United States of America
08 07 06 05 04   5 4 3 2 1
First edition

Contents

Foreword

The eminent New Testament scholar Martin Hengel once noted that the rapid missionary expansion of early Christianity was not the result of a triumphant and compelling idea but of the compelling witness of extraordinary people.

In many ways, that is the underlying message of this exceptional book by Elizabeth Browne. In her former work, *The Disabled Disciple* (Liguori, 1997), she probed the biblical and theological foundations for an inclusive Church, one that would welcome all of God's children.

In that book, too, her theology was illustrated by wonderful stories of people who embodied what she was talking about. Now, in this follow-up publication she treats her readers to more of those great testimonies that show people of faith who are overcoming obstacles to be an integral part of the Christian community and the human family.

This book has a practical, how-to spin that is a clear reflection of its author. Elizabeth describes a series of workshops that help other people of good will understand the experience of persons with disabilities and why access and inclusion are so important. I am touched and pleased that she refers by way of illustration to a series of workshops for graduate students in ministry that take place at Catholic Theological Union. It has always been a joy for me to take part in those sessions. But what Elizabeth in her modesty does not reveal is that she herself is the heart and soul of these educational experiences. Her transparent honesty, her always gracious spirit, and her hard-won credibility as a great teacher, a creative theologian, and an absorbing storyteller leave an indelible imprint on her students.

The contents of this book also bear her imprint, and readers will be blessed to encounter it. What she describes here is not simply a strategy to deal with an important pastoral issue but a vision of the church that reflects the spirit of Jesus who came to call all people, and especially those pushed to the margins, to a life of communion and grace.

DONALD SENIOR, C.P.
CATHOLIC THEOLOGICAL UNION AT CHICAGO

Preface

In my previous book, *The Disabled Disciple* (Liguori Publications, 1997), I noted that ministries involving persons with disabilities are being implemented in many churches and denominations. Those ministries offer hope for countless people who previously have been overlooked, ignored, and dismissed as unworthy of serious attention for far too long.

Especially gratifying to me were the positive responses I received about the book from individuals with disabilities. Those responses are affirmations of the work I have begun. They also communicated the joy these respondents felt because at last one of their very own was speaking out about concerns that had troubled them for years. Though others have spoken about the plight of persons with disabilities, here is one of their own who had something significant to say.

Some suggested that every bishop in the United States should read the book. (I rather liked that idea.) Many were forthright in noting their discouragement because of the condescending attitudes of many church leaders toward people with disabilities. They felt dismissed as irreligious or ignored as malcontents whenever they raised issues over the treatment of individuals with disabilities in today's Church.

Another positive response came from a national organization comprised of various religious denominations that formed the National Association of the Blind in Communities of Faith. In 2000, they invited me to address the organization at the National Federation of the Blind (NFB) annual convention in Atlanta. Several had also commented on my article, "Challenging Biblical Stereotypes of the Blind," published in the February 1998 issue of *The Braille Monitor*, Volume 41, No. 2 (a publication of the NFB). They spoke, not surprisingly, of similar unacceptable attitudes toward persons with disabilities within their different denominations. We agreed that we need a clearer understanding not only of Scripture but also of the significance of the roles we assign to people with disabilities in our churches.

Many of the comments I received in response to *The Disabled Disciple* were at first surprising. They did not refer to any deep theological understandings of Christian teaching or practice which I had considered the foundations of my reflections. (In fact, those insights were scarcely noted!) Instead, most respondents talked about the stories and anecdotes that added clarity or illustrated a point, even though those were merely personal accounts of feeling excluded or included. Comments were usually along these lines:

- "Tell more of those stories about all the people you have met."
- "I never realized what people were feeling, or how people were reacting to what I simply took for granted as a practicing Christian."
- "I have never met people like the ones you write about. Tell us more of those stories."

So stories it will be!

Andrew Greeley, a researcher and Catholic author, says that stories are the primary means by which human beings come to understand their own reality. People also relate better to their own reality through telling their stories. And the better the story, the more accurate grasp one has of reality. Some would even say that stories are the most effective means of handing on our traditions and heritage to succeeding generations.

So, not surprisingly, stories have become the main point of departure for my work of fostering inclusion, and I realize how significant that focus is. After all, many fine theologians are carefully at work analyzing the doctrines and foundations of our faith. But the stories contained here are from people, many of whom have not been part of mainstream religious society at all. Yet, these ordinary—and not so ordinary—individuals share a wisdom from experience that provides insight into living our common faith.

Everyone must be made aware that persons who are different in any way are often excluded from our churches. Our focus here is to bring about a transformation—a true *metanoia*—to that situation. Thus, this book offers reflections with examples and concrete suggestions on building ministry for persons with disabilities. An additional aim of this book is to offer a deeper understanding of the skills and processes needed to implement and further develop those ministries where they have already been implemented. We may not arrive at the ultimate solution for everyone, but we must attempt to move toward one. Through such efforts, we begin to build the kingdom of God in our midst.

But, how shall we carry all this out? To share, we must gather and invite others to gather with us. We must break bread and call one another by name. We must get to know one another and begin to understand one another. That is what I hope to accomplish through this book.

I Had Been Hungry

I had been hungry, all the Years—
My Noon had Come—to dine—
I trembling drew the Table near—
And touched the Curious Wine—

'Twas this on Tables I had seen—
When turning, hungry, Home,
I looked in Windows, for the Wealth
I could not hope—for Mine—

I did not know the ample Bread—
'Twas so unlike the Crumb
The Birds and I, had often shared
In Nature's—Dining Room—

The Plenty hurt me—'twas so new—
Myself felt ill—and odd—
As Berry—of a Mountain Bush—
Transplanted—to a Road—

Nor was I hungry—so I found
That Hunger—was a way
Of Persons outside Windows—
The Entering—takes away—

EMILY DICKINSON, LXXVI (579)

CHAPTER ONE

Inclusion

The Mark of True Acceptance

*The greatest obstacle to love is fear. It has been the source
of all defects in human behavior throughout the ages.*
MAHMOUD MOHAMED TAHA

A sixty-six-year-old double amputee waiting for a plane at a busy U.S. airport has been perched on top of a baggage cart "like a sack of potatoes." He is finally wheeled onto a plane and left there for more than thirty minutes while other passengers stare at him. At another airport, a disability rights activist dressed in a business suit sits in a wheelchair awaiting her flight. Another businesswoman walks up and drops a quarter in her coffee cup.

These are not some isolated instances of discrimination against people with disabilities in the United States, but examples of how mainstream culture treats those who are disabled—even today as we begin a new century. Pervasive prejudices against persons with disabilities infect both the public and private sectors of American society, and many persons, even those who are well-meaning, do not recognize the damaging nature of prejudice against those with disabilities.

Dealing with a person who is disabled is often a fearful encounter for those who have no previous experience in handling such situations. Though many people are eager to overcome their fear of heights or flying or visiting someone who is terminally ill ("I might catch something," they worry), large numbers of folks who consider

1

themselves without disabilities make little effort to overcome their fear of facing a person in a wheelchair, or one who has a visual impairment, or one who has a hearing loss.

An antidote to these fears is faith and love. God knows that we need courage, and courage is ours. It can belong to all of us if we face our fears and open our hearts and minds.

Jesus asks, "Why are you afraid? Have you no faith?" (Mk 4:40).

As we read in the first epistle of John, "There is no fear in love" (1 Jn 4:18). We are people who want to love just as Jesus loved. He welcomed all who came to him. And yet each of us fears the unknown, the outsider, the foreigner, the different ones who appear in our midst. When they seek to join our safe and comfortable communities, we inwardly ask, "Why don't they stay in their own place, with their own kind, where they can feel at ease?" But if we fear (and all of us fear something), then in the mind of John, we do not truly love as our Lord loved.

In the following poem, the Jesuit poet, Gerard Manley Hopkins, speaks to a child named Margaret who weeps over the fallen leaves of autumn, inwardly sensing that it is not just the end of bright summer days, but that all things pass away.

Spring and Fall
to a young child

MÁRGARÉT, áre you gríeving
Over Goldengrove unleaving?
Leáves, líke the things of man, you
With your fresh thoughts care for, can you?
Áh! ás the heart grows older
It will come to such sights colder
By and by, nor spare a sigh
Though worlds of wanwood leafmeal lie;
And yet you wíll weep and know why.
Now no matter, child, the name:
Sórrow's springs áre the same.

Nor mouth had, no nor mind, expressed
What heart heard of, ghost guessed:
It is the blight man was born for,
It is Margaret you mourn for.
GERARD MANLEY HOPKINS (31)

Margaret weeps, and we weep with her, avoiding our real fear by poetically consoling a little child in her grief at falling leaves. Margaret—or you and I—all weep as leaves fall and as friends die. But it is not really the fall of leaves or the death of loved ones for which we weep. It is our own vulnerability that we mourn. We wonder, "If leaves fall and friends die, then why not us as well?"

Humans have known fear since the beginning of time. Our ancient cave parents huddled close to bright fires in order to fend off wild beasts and other unknown elements that lurked beyond the entrances to their safe caverns. Today, people with disabilities often are those foreign, or at least discomfort-causing elements, outside the boundaries of our personal safety zones. A twisted and contorted body strapped in a wheelchair, a clumsy blind man with a long white cane, or a deaf woman unaware of people speaking to her from behind— all these cause our inner alarms to sound, "Thank God that is not me!"

Based on a Harris Survey entitled "Americans With Disabilities" and conducted in 2000, the National Catholic Partnership on Disabilities estimates that over *fourteen million* Catholics in the United States have one or more disabilities. Perhaps the 1978 *Pastoral Statement of the U.S. Catholic Bishops on People With Disabilities* (see Appendix D for complete text) can shed some light on our current discussion about our fear of inclusion. The bishops wrote:

What individuals with disabilities need, first of all, is acceptance in this difference that can neither be denied nor overlooked. No acts of charity or of justice can be of lasting value unless our actions are informed by a sincere and understanding love that penetrates the wall of strangeness and affirms the common humanity underlying all distinction (para. 3).

Inclusion is not a newly revealed concept. We find in ancient Isaiah an invitation to feel welcome at God's table.

> *Everyone who thirsts, come to the waters;*
> *and you that have no money, come, buy and eat!*
> *Come, buy wine and milk without money*
> *and without price…*
> *Listen carefully to me, and eat what is good,*
> *and delight yourselves in rich food.*
>
> ISAIAH 55:1–2

In this passage, Isaiah reaches out to the alienated ones, promising them a seat at the table just as Emily Dickinson (in her poem on the page 2 of this chapter) welcomed those feasting on crumbs to share the ample bread and curious wine as full members of the community. Isaiah's welcoming call to inclusion is clear. He summons us to openness, and to ensure that all share the banquet with its rich foods and fine wines. God calls us to drink of the refreshing waters without cost. How that must have cheered the beleaguered wanderers in the deserts of those ancient times! The prophet sent out that invitation long ago, and God has been awaiting our response.

Jesus first announced his mission in the synagogue of his hometown as he unrolled the scroll and read these words, also from Isaiah:

> *The spirit of the Lord is upon me,*
> *because he has anointed me*
> *to bring glad news to the poor.*
> *He has sent me to proclaim release*
> *to the captives*
> *and recovery of sight to the blind,*
> *to let the oppressed go free,*
> *to proclaim the year of the Lord's favor.*
>
> LUKE 4:18–19

In his own life, Jesus shows how this is to be done. He reached out to all persons—foreigners, women, tax collectors, prostitutes, the blind, the deaf, and the lame. All were welcomed. Jesus' life provides abundant examples, and he instructs us in parables on how we are to carry out his mission. Like any good rabbi (a word that means "teacher"), whenever people came to Jesus with questions, problems, or challenges, he told stories by way of explanation.

For example, when asked, "And who is my neighbor?" Jesus replied with this story:

> *A man was going down from Jerusalem to Jericho, and fell into the hands of robbers, who stripped him, beat him, and went away, leaving him half dead....But a Samaritan while traveling came near him; and when he saw him, he was moved with pity. He went to him and bandaged his wounds, having poured oil and wine on them. Then he put him on his own animal, brought him to an inn, and took care of him. The next day he took out two denarii, gave them to the innkeeper, and said, "Take care of him; and when I come back, I will repay you whatever more you spend."*
>
> LUKE 10:30–35

Yes, God has left us a command, and Jesus has given us the example; now we need only accept the grace to follow his way. The intent of these pages is to foster greater awareness of the importance of inclusion in every area of our community, especially in our religious culture. Therefore, the first challenge is to demonstrate how necessary it is that persons with disabilities be included in the development of inclusion programs. Only they can provide suitable sensitivity and proper perspectives to make the ministry successful. We must move from theoretical theology toward a working reality that will empower individuals with disabilities to be included fully in our religious communities.

Whether at Isaiah's banquet with its fine wines, the Samaritan's hospitality at the inn, or Emily Dickinson's table with its ample bread, the result will surely begin to alleviate spiritual hunger and thirst. We pray that we can respond to God's open invitation to a banquet where all are truly welcomed.

Interacting With People Who Have Disabilities

The 1990 passage of the Americans With Disabilities Act gives all of us greater opportunities to be involved in situations where people with disabilities are present. Many of us cling to our fears or feel awkward in such situations. This is partly due to our lack of positive experience with people with physical or mental disabilities. Most of us want to be polite and helpful, but many of us make mistakes based on our ingrained stereotypes, fear of awkwardness in social and work situations, or a desire to avoid those we do not consider "normal."

The following section offers some advice in the hopes that, with practice, we all can do better. A good first step in thinking inclusively is to realize the people with disabilities experience individual thoughts and emotions, have the same needs as other folks, and should not be thought of as objects of condescending over-compassion or examples of heroic achievement. They are people like you and like me. A good key to dealing with people who are disabled is to communicate with respect and keep your actions as similar in tone and tenor to those that would take place in your ordinary everyday interactions.

Here are some tips to support you when you first meet someone with a disability:

1. Take a proactive stand and introduce yourself, especially if some-one else is not doing so. Include the person in the group's conversation; do not leave the person on the periphery, but welcome him or her into the group.
2. Offer a handshake as a sign of politeness, respect, and equal inclusion. Offer your hand, even if you don't think that the person can grasp it. If the person does not respond to your offer of a handshake, quietly drop your hand to your side. In the case of

someone who cannot see, lightly touch his or her hand. Exercise common sense, and ask if you are unsure.

3. Make eye contact just as you would with anyone else. Do not let your gaze wander about the room or the area, implying that the person, even if sighted, will be unaware of your lack of full attention.

4. Proceed with the conversation as you would with any new acquaintance. Do not assume that the person who is disabled has few friends. Instead make an effort to get to know him or her. The effort may be especially rewarding.

5. Speak clearly and face to face when talking to someone with a hearing impairment.

Here is some practical advice on getting to know a person with disabilities:

1. See people as individuals with a particular set of God-given talents. Make a genuine effort to get to know them. Often, people with disabilities are left feeling that no one really wants to interact with them on a deeper-than-superficial level. We have all been given different gifts by God, some of them not so apparent at first meeting. Give people with disabilities the same chance you would give in seeking friendship with others.

2. Think about the person with disabilities as a full participant in a friendship. No matter what our human strengths or weaknesses, we are all interdependent and can learn from one another.

3. Use basic good manners and common sense. For example, if you have a blind neighbor, say "hello" in a normal voice, even if you think that the person won't know who you are. Lightly touch the blind person's arm and introduce yourself, just as you would with a seeing person.

4. Ask the person with disabilities directly how you can be of assistance. This may be difficult with people who have cognitive disabilities, but we can teach ourselves to patiently deal with those who have some trouble making their needs known.

5. Do not automatically speak for someone who has disabilities, even if others are having difficulty understanding what is being said. If a disabled person accepts your offer of help, speak to that person directly, asking questions and confirming what was said until it is clear.

6. A quiet offer of "May I help you?" is a good first step when you see a disabled person struggling. Perhaps the person wants help, but perhaps he or she also wants to accomplish the task in question on their own.

7. All disabled people do not have the same needs. Just because you have experienced a person with a particular disability who wants a particular kind of help doesn't mean that all persons with disabilities have that same need.

8. Remember that people with disabilities of whatever kind or to whatever degree want basically to be seen as full citizens of society, both secular and religious.

9. Interact with a disabled person as a healthy person. An individual is not automatically sick just because he or she has a functional disability. Some disabilities do not have accompanying health consequences.

10. Keep uppermost in your mind that disabled people must complete the same tasks of daily living as you do. Many people with disabilities find it extremely difficult to get a salesperson to wait on them in stores or to get a cab to stop for them. Keep in mind that disabled individuals are customers, patrons, and audiences, and deserve equal attention when shopping, traveling, dining, or attending sporting, theatrical, and religious events.

Many attitudinal barriers exist in the minds of the nondisabled. These practices and suggestions can help alleviate the fears and soften attitudes.

Questions for
Reflection and Discussion

1. If you were the double amputee left on the baggage cart, how would you respond? How would you go about achieving respectful assistance?
2. If you were the woman in a wheelchair who was thoughtlessly given a "handout" of money in her coffee cup, how would you respond? How would you be tempted to respond?
3. Here is a definition of disability from the Americans With Disabilities Act. Would you expand that definition? Would you add more categories?

"The ADA applies to persons who have impairments and that these must substantially limit major life activities, such as seeing, hearing, speaking, walking, breathing, performing manual tasks, learning, caring for oneself, and working. An individual with epilepsy, paralysis, HIV infection, AIDS, a substantial hearing or visual impairment, mental retardation, or a specific learning disability is covered, but an individual with a minor, nonchronic condition of short duration, such as a sprain, broken limb, or the flu, generally would not be covered."

Challenge

1. If you had to choose to be disabled, what disability would you select? Why?
2. What disability do you already have—even though it may not be obvious to others? Do you need eyeglasses, for example? Do you need insulin to treat diabetes? Do you have a bad back from a sports injury?

CHAPTER TWO

The Workshop

Model for Fostering Inclusion

"And…he had been made known to them in the breaking of the bread."

LUKE 24:35

As part of my work at Catholic Theological Union in Chicago, I have helped develop workshops on inclusion that have been presented to ordained and soon-to-be ordained ministers whose ministries will inevitably include disabled individuals of all descriptions. These workshops proved to be a valuable and effective strategy in addressing the challenges which such ministers will encounter. The workshop model also offers a formula readily adaptable to a parish situation where members are striving to break down barriers within their worshiping community.

The advantage of such a workshop, developed and presented by individuals who have disabilities, is that it provides an opportunity for comradeship, direct communication, friendship, and for a grassroots sort of communication that may be absent in some other approach. It is the model I suggest to parishes/communities who want to initiate a program of inclusion.

Pattern of the Workshop

The pattern of the workshop has proven simple to organize. It is easily expandable and adjustable to different ideas as new groups of participants listen to and share insights with an ever-changing panel of up to six individuals. The panelists, all with various disabilities, volunteer to share their stories, provide their expertise, and respond to questions. Each member of the panel is a practicing Christian, willing to candidly address the successes as well as the awkwardness experienced in dealing with their own communities of faith—and with the world at large.

First, while registration takes place, the "bread and the wine" is shared—the coffee is poured, and the cakes are broken. This essential human activity of drinking and eating together begins to dismantle the wall of strangeness that separates us from one another. It works much like the bread shared with the stranger on the road to Emmaus who walked along with the two disciples as they fled the chaos in Jerusalem on that first post-Resurrection morning.

Then, each panelist makes a presentation to the whole group, based on his or her unique experience. They present stories of personal experiences in regard to their own disabilities, and give honest accounts of how they have been excluded from or welcomed into their own communities.

Next, the workshop participants break out into small groups, each moderated by one of the panelists. These smaller forums allow participants to gather in a specific group reflecting his or her own particular desire to learn more about the issues of persons with that specific disability. Questions and discussions cover a wide spectrum from "How do you handle this or that physical challenge?" to some rather surprising queries, such as "Why would you want to do that?" and "Aren't you overwhelmed by your disability?"

In this smaller venue, participants feel more at ease. Their hearts have been warmed by sharing food and drink, by now they know names and faces, and the frank remarks from the panel of presenters have dispelled their fear. Here they are more able to ask questions, seek specific information, and thus acquire personal insights into challenges faced by individuals with disabilities. They can also reflect on how best the community might erase barriers to accommodating all people.

Finally, the whole group reassembles to share ideas from the small group sessions, and discuss them to whatever extent seems appropriate. At the end, each participant is asked to evaluate the experience.

The structure is that simple. Of course, its success depends on the effectiveness of the presenters' comments and on the openness of the participants to be profoundly changed by the experience.

In recent sessions, we have included a video presentation of Cardinal Joseph Bernardin's convocation "That All May Worship," held in Chicago in 1996. This inclusive liturgy was developed during the last few months of the Cardinal's life. It was his effort to bring all of his flock—those with disabilities and those without—into a shared liturgical worship service. Participants at our workshops have been especially impressed by the inclusion of mentally handicapped persons as well as the physically disabled in the liturgy video.

Incidently, the most frequent request we receive is for copies of the video, along with questions about how it came into being. Not long afterward, another video was prepared in which a Jewish boy with cerebral palsy prepares for his bar mitzvah. Thus, efforts toward inclusion of persons with disabilities has also become a value among members of the Jewish community.

Workshop Evaluations

At the end of each of these workshops, we ask for evaluations from the participants. One very thoughtful minister sent me a taped evaluation because she wanted me to hear her own words rather than have someone read them to me. She said she had been working in ministry with the disabled for twenty years and had never before seen such joy, humor, or laughter among participants as they interacted with the panelists and exchanged ideas that night. "I will no longer work in this ministry with the pity, fear, and regret that I had before, praying for a miracle to restore someone's sight, hearing, or mobility. Now I will begin to appreciate what we can gain from accepting each other as we are."

I appreciated her sensitivity in sending her comments on tape so I could hear them myself. It was further evidence that she really got the message of exclusion persons feel who are blind and always need someone to read their personal notes. I vividly remember the relief I felt when I started using a scanner to read personal letters and memos from professional colleagues because, if my work was being rejected, I wanted to know *first* so I could prepare for the comments of others.

At another workshop, I was the final presenter and, exhausted, I stepped outside to get some fresh air. A participant followed me and asked to speak with me. She was a Native American from Thunder Bay, Ontario, Canada, a member of the Ojibwa tribe. She said that she had something special to give me. I started to object, thinking it was some tangible token. But leaning against the warm stones of the building, I joyfully received her gift: a song in her native language, normally sung to the dawn or to a tiny child. That night, she sang it for me. I have not the words, nor can I duplicate their meaning, but the sound of her clear voice remains in my soul.

Earlier during the discussion period, she had told us of a mentally retarded man who "wanders all around from town to town in northern Ontario." He travels by air since that is the only way to get from place to place. No one ever questions him. No one asks for tickets or fares, and he finds lodging and food wherever he journeys. He is perfectly safe, always free, and is treated as one of the blessed ones, touched by God. He is simply one of the strangers all of us pass by on our journey home."

In the same group, a director of religious education from Indianapolis became wholeheartedly committed to the concept of inclusion and brought back to the bishop and priests of her archdiocese what she discovered.

Another participant remarked that the workshop helped him realize that it need not be complicated for parishes to make it possible for all to be included. The most important values, he maintains, is for pastors and ministers to be aware of what they can do to foster inclusion, of how important it is for ministers of hospitality and ushers to be sensitive to all members of the parish, and of the need for participation by persons with disabilities in parish planning processes.

Setting Up a Parish Workshop to Foster Inclusion

While workshops offered by educational institutions such as the Catholic Theological Union are often set up by professionals, this method may also be used with good results at a parish or neighborhood level. Following are some general guidelines for organizing such a learning experience.

The Panel of Presenters: Persons from the parish and/or neighborhood whom people will recognize are the best choice as presenters. As an alternative, the diocesan office with responsibility for encouraging ministry to the disabled may be able to suggest other available local speakers. Information and representatives from local chapters of organizations listed in the Appendix of this book might also be asked to attend, or at least may be helpful in recommending names of possible panelists. (See Appendix C, page 101.) Volunteers should be assigned to provide transportation, necessary equipment, and initial hospitality for each presenter.

Attendees: Special effort should be made to ensure maximum attendance at this workshop. Preliminary advertising should include such considerations as contacting churches in the immediate area, announcements or fliers in parish bulletins, and small press releases to editors who cover religious affairs for local newspapers. Arrangements should also be made to include a variety of age ranges and genders.

Program Content: A parish committee may be formed to host and plan this first event. Representatives of people with different disabilities *must be included in the planning.* It may be wise for this committee to devise simple, observable behavioral goals for the outcome of this workshop. A brief outline of the content may be prepared, but panelists also must always feel free to offer their particular insights.

Planners should attend to the administrative issues involved with such a workshop: place, length of program, breaks, location of rest rooms and telephones, refreshments, the building's smoking policy, and so on. The workshop space must also be checked for size, accessibility, seating arrangement, noise, lighting, and electrical outlets. Chalkboards, easels, markers, overhead projectors, and other needed supplies must be procured ahead of time. Handouts for the group should be created, as well as any simulated exercises such as a blindfolded trust-walk.

Program Evaluation

A simple feedback sheet may be provided for those who attend. The following list gives some typical areas that may be addressed on a workshop evaluation form:

- Were the objectives met?
- Were questions encouraged and sufficiently answered?
- Rate each presenters' ability to provide necessary information.
- List the ideas and terminology new to each participant.
- How do you rate the overall organization of workshop, including schedule of the day?
- Give a brief summary of new knowledge gained.
- How would you rate the comfort and accessibility of the physical facilities?

It may also be helpful to include a few open-ended questions that do not involve a lengthy response, for example: What did you find most valuable about this workshop?" or "What would you wish to change?"

Producing Large-Print Information

In setting up a workshop of this type, and in other situations as well, it may be helpful to have some guidelines for producing large-print information. These are given in an effort to make printed text more accessible.

- Use 16 point type or above, or test out the type size and face beforehand on potential readers to see which they prefer.
- Do not use more than two different print sizes in a single document since this may cause confusion to the reader.
- Use plain-style fonts without excessive loops or swashes. Plain fonts are easier to read.
- Do not fully justify a text; a ragged right-hand margin makes reading easier.
- Do not indent paragraphs; instead leave extra space between them.
- Avoid using BLOCK CAPITALS: These are difficult to read.
- Do not place text over the top of graphics.
- Make sure that page numbers, headings, and captions for photographs are also in large print.
- To emphasize words either enlarge the print size further or put in bold-faced type. Do not underline the text.
- Avoid using more than one column per page; this may disorient the reader.
- Use light-colored matte paper, or a paper with a good contrast, such as black print on a light-yellow paper.
- Avoid glossy paper since the glare can cause confusion.

- If large-print documents are bulky, comb binding them is generally better than stapling. Alternately, you may wish to insert the material into a binder of adequate size.

An Abundant Harvest

Experience with this workshop is a positive one of consciousness-raising and attitude change. It is hoped that this model will be of widespread benefit to parishes across the country. The harvest of creating a parish with a soul of inclusion is abundant. In the following chapters, persons with disabilities share personal stories that may prompt increased learning and understanding among all.

Questions for Reflection and Discussion

1. If you were in charge of a workshop for inclusion, what arrangements would you be most careful about? What kind of adaptations might be necessary for panelists?
2. If you were in charge of this workshop for inclusion, what personal preparations would you make? If you were to distribute a package of materials in advance, what would you include in this package to help ensure the success of this workshop?

Challenge

1. Imagine that you are jockey Bill Shoemaker, winner of more than eight thousand horse races, who retired after winning the Kentucky Derby at age fifty-four, only to become a paraplegic in an automobile accident. What obstacles might you have to overcome, both physically and emotionally?
2. Discuss the following incident, using the questions that follow as a basis for discussion:

A professor had applied for a position in the English department of a highly regarded women's college. She did not mention that she was blind. Late in the summer, shortly before classes were to start, she received a phone call from the department chair, offering a meeting to disucss a position as an adjunct professor. The woman was perplexed. Should she follow the advice of some career counselors and "take charge," telling the prospective employer forthrightly about her disability.

She returned the phone call and suggested an immediate interview. "That's not necessary," the chair replied. "Your résumé speaks precisely to what we need and what we want right now. Just sign the contract and come ahead to class. We can get together right afterward for coffee and a chat. Your qualifications suit us to perfection."

After the department chair hung up, the professor reflected that this response was just what should happen—in an ideal world. But, at this time of indecision, she decided to phone her employer once more and tell all.

"Oh," she said tentatively, "I thought you should know that I use a guide dog, and I was wondering if that would be a problem?"

The chair replied enthusiastically, "How wonderful to have a dog on campus. I'm so looking forward to meeting you after your class, which will be this Monday at 9:00 A.M. Just pick up your contract at the front desk, sign it, and pop it into my mail slot. See you then."

1. Would you respond as the department chair did if you were in her place?
2. Have you ever considered hiring a person with a disability?
3. Which kind of disability would you find most acceptable for your particular replacement on the job or in parish ministry?
4. If you have ever worked with a disabled individual, what was that experience like for you and others around you?

CHAPTER THREE

Susan's Story

Bold and Faithful

My life is spent with sorrow,
and my years with sighing;
my strength fails because of my misery,
and my bones waste away....
But I trust in you, O LORD;
I say, "You are my God."
My times are in your hand."

PSALM 32:9–10, 14–15

Susan was one of the most enthusiastic of our presenters, easily winning the full attention of the participants. She embodies the spirit of the words "Bold and Faithful," which are emblazoned over the front door of the Catholic Theological Union where this workshop took place.

Like many individuals in the parables who, despite objections from the onlookers and even from his own disciples, Susan was drawn to Jesus, seeking his healing touch and understanding words. She reminded me of people from the parables who felt power coming forth from Jesus, knowing he cared for them and would heal their wounded souls and bodies.

In one of the parables, a leper, filled with faith, boldly approached Jesus, ringing his bell to announce his presence. "Unclean, unclean!" he cried. Kneeling down, he addressed Jesus saying, "Lord, if you choose, you can make me clean." And, of course, Jesus stretched out

19

his hand and touched him and said, "I do choose. Be made clean!" (Mt 8:2–3).

Another time crowds tried in vain to silence a noisy blind man begging at the side of a road on which Jesus was passing. He shouted out, "Jesus, son of David, have mercy on me!" And the people tried to silence him, but he would not be denied. Jesus stopped and waited for the man to draw near, and said to him, "What do you want me to do for you?" And the beggar said, *"Domine, ut videam!"* ("Lord, that I may see!"). And, Jesus cured him. (See Mk 10:46–52.)

Even a Syrophoenician woman, not of the Jewish faith, the mother of a sick child, kept following after Jesus, crying out for him to have pity on her daughter. Jesus stopped, despite the pleading of the disciples, "Send her away, for she keeps shouting after us!" Marveling at her courage and boldness, he said (and he must have been smiling), "Woman, great is your faith! Let it be done for you as you wish." (See Mt 15:21–28.)

In Spite of the Difficulties

Susan had the same kind of faith and determination found in those Gospel stories. Although Susan was born with cerebral palsy and used Canadian crutches (forearm crutches rather than under-the-arm crutches) for mobility, she knew that she was fully capable of becoming involved in reaping the harvest that is ripening in the field. She was very aware of the many programs set up to enable young volunteers to provide services in inner cities throughout our country. She wanted to join one and share her own talents after college.

Religious communities have long supported such lay groups, encouraging college students to spend a year or more living and working with the poor in American cities as well as in underdeveloped countries. The Jesuit Volunteer Corps was one of the earliest of such Catholic volunteer organizations. Other religious communities—Lutherans, Maronites, Presbyterians, and so on—support similar groups. These thriving organizations are a real tribute to the youth in our country. If the volunteers wish, the supporting religious groups provide spiritual direction, guidance, and support to these dedicated young people as appropriate.

So, upon graduation, Susan applied to several programs, but was rejected by each. She persisted, however, and was finally accepted into the Passionist Lay Missioners (PLMs), becoming one of the best volunteers the program ever had. Assigned to work in the Uptown neighborhood of Chicago, Susan began her ministry with enthusiasm and professional capability. It was there that I had the good fortune of getting to know her and rejoicing at how readily she was accepted into this new PLM community.

Along with five other volunteers, she moved into a fifth floor apartment on Kenmore Avenue with her boxes and bags—but no elevator. Soon she took on her part of the responsibilities of community living with new friends—other college graduates from all over the world. Each of the six members shared duties by taking turns dividing up the chores. At first, Susan had cleaning responsibility for the front room, bathroom, and hallway.

Each member also had an opportunity to cook meals for the others. Daily the community joined in prayer and social activities together. Each one worked full time at his or her own particular assignment, as well as teaching, assisting at a homeless shelter, undertaking prison visits, and so on. In addition, the group enjoyed getting away for retreat times during their year's commitment.

Susan's ministry was teaching English at an alternative high school—essentially a school program for students who were not making it in the public-school system. Slight of build but formidable of spirit, she began her day by clambering up three flights of stairs to her classroom in the dilapidated structure where the school was located (having just climbed down from the fifth-floor PLM community apartment!). These feats were all accomplished daily. Nothing seemed to stop her. Neither snow nor ice—as only Chicagoans know snow and ice—could keep her from her classes.

She taught short stories and English grammar and, on the side, taught about herself by caring for these marginal students. She even confronted the Chicago police department as they rushed in one morning, guns drawn, on a routine Chicago drug bust. She asked them to give notice next time, because they were disrupting her class.

Commenting on little incidents that had occurred in her local parish, she recounted the time she volunteered to be a eucharistic minister. Someone asked, "Did people accept you?" "No problem," she said. "I would just stare people down if they tried to avoid my line when it was my turn to distribute Christ's body and blood." She refused to be set aside, but stepped forward and assumed a position which she would not let be denied her.

Many of the stories in the Bible offer similar examples of deep faith, such as the sick and the outcast who persist in approaching Jesus for his saving touch, even in spite of the complaints of his disciples. "Send her away, for she keeps shouting after us!" Susan, and all the others in these stories have one significant characteristic in common: they are bold and faithful, and have a true sense of their own worth, which must never "be denied" them. (See Acts 19:36.)

What Is Cerebral Palsy?

Cerebral palsy is a condition in which the motor control areas of the brain are permanently damaged. This movement disorder usually occurs before, during, or shortly after birth. There are many possible causes of this condition; premature babies and babies born during multiple births have a higher risk of having cerebral palsy than other babies. For some people, the symptoms of cerebral palsy start in early infancy; for others, the symptoms do not arise until early childhood.

People with cerebral palsy have poor muscle control and coordination. Their arms or legs may have spastic, or tight and stiff, muscles. Their body may move in abnormal ways, and their balance may be poor as well. They also may have difficulty speaking or swallowing.

Cerebral palsy affects different people differently, depending on how much of the brain is damaged or the location of the damage. For example, the only symptom of one person with mild cerebral palsy is a slight limp. Another with severe cerebral palsy cannot walk, talk, or read and cannot hold her head up, sit up, or use her hands. The Irish artist-writer Christy Brown, who was featured in the movie *My Left Foot*, could only control that one part of his body. He used his left foot to paint remarkable pictures.

People with cerebral palsy may have additional problems, including seizures, mental retardation, vision or hearing loss, or possible emotional problems.

True or False

There are many misconceptions about cerebral palsy and its resulting disabilities. Go over these true/false statements to see if you hold any of those misconceptions.

1. *Cerebral palsy can be cured.* False: Once the brain has been damaged, it does not repair itself. Cerebral palsy is a lifelong condition.
2. *Cerebral palsy is contagious.* False: It cannot be spread from one person to another like a cold or the flu. It is also not a genetic disease, that is, one that is inherited.
3. *All people with cerebral palsy are mentally retarded.* False. Most people with cerebral palsy have normal intelligence. The tragic consequences of this myth can be seen in the story of Ruth Sienkiewicz-Mercer whose cerebral palsy left her unable to speak. She was diagnosed as severely mentally retarded at age five. Ruth spent her childhood in state hospitals for the retarded. One day, an aide noticed that Ruth laughed at a humorous story. Hospital officials discovered that Ruth was not retarded at all.
4. *Some treatments can help people with cerebral palsy to improve their movements.* True: Physical therapists can train people in sitting, balancing, and walking. They can also improve a person's muscle tone and posture as well as advise on the use of braces, crutches, wheelchairs, and other aids.

Questions for Reflection and Discussion

1. What gifts would a person like Susan bring to any volunteer program or ministry at your parish?
2. How could you help parishioners respond positively to a young person with cerebral palsy—someone like Susan with crutches—who volunteers for a very visible ministry position in your parish?
3. Have you ever known anyone who has cerebral palsy? What was your initial reaction?
4. Imagine that you have difficulty controlling your muscles. What activities of daily life would be difficult for you?
5. While physical limitations can be significant in cases of cerebral palsy, social concerns are equally daunting, as noted by this person with CP:

I think people in general have a harder time dealing with a person with CP than they do with people with other disabilities. It may be because of a number of things like the spastic movements, the drooling, or the lack of communication. I don't think the world as a whole views people with CP as very pretty people, but that's because they don't see beyond the outside."

GARY KARP, *LIFE ON WHEELS* (SEBASTOPOL, CA: O'REILLY, 1999)

Would you agree or disagree with this statement? What was your first reaction to seeing a person with cerebral palsy?

Challenge

1. Put yourself in the role of those who tried avoiding Susan's Communion line. Perhaps role play the situation. Reflect on your feelings upon first seeing her there.
2. Try to surmise the issues that are behind people's avoidance of a person like Susan in church or in any public volunteer program.

CHAPTER FOUR

Margaret's Story

Breaking and Entering

But all things are possible with God.
MATTHEW 19:26

Margaret's story which she presented to our workshop reminded me of the following story about Jesus and the paralytic.

> *When he [Jesus] returned to Capernaum after some days, it was reported that he was at home. So many gathered around that there was no longer room for them, not even in front of the door; and he was speaking the word to them.*
>
> *Then some people came, bringing to him a paralyzed man, carried by four of them. And when they could not bring him to Jesus because of the crowd, they removed the roof above him; and after having dug through it, they let down the mat on which the paralytic lay. When Jesus saw their faith, he said to the paralytic, "Son, your sins are forgiven."*
>
> *Now some of the scribes were sitting there, questioning in their hearts, "Why does this fellow speak in this way? It is blasphemy! Who can forgive sins but God alone?" At once Jesus perceived in his spirit that they were discussing these questions among themselves; and he said to them, "Why do you raise such questions in your hearts? Which is easier, to say to the paralytic, 'Your sins are forgiven,' or to say, 'Stand up and take your mat and walk'?*

But so that you may know that the Son of Man has au-
thority on earth to forgive sins"—he said to the paralytic—"I
say to you, stand up, take your mat, and go to your home." And
he stood up, and immediately took the mat and went out be-
fore all of them.

MARK 2:3–12

Those friends of the paralyzed man creatively devised an opportunity to get someone to Jesus who could not squeeze through the
crowd, much like the presenter Margaret who was at another of our
workshops. Margaret, who is wheelchair bound, would like to have
been involved in the activities of her busy and active parish, but she
had never been invited, and she saw no ready way of squeezing herself into the crowded parish schedules.

One day, however, she responded to a notice in the bulletin re-
questing religious educators for the catechism classes that met on
Saturdays. Inwardly, she doubted that she would be accepted, though
she knew she was fully qualified for that role. "No harm in trying,"
she thought, "I've been rejected before. So I simply applied to teach
catechism classes on Saturday morning. I was accepted, and an entire
ministry opened up for me. Now I am chair of the liturgy committee
and I'm on the parish council. Perhaps I get a little overextended
from time to time, but I love it. I am a functional part of the community, and I know my participation is valued and appreciated."

Margaret understands the importance of our disability workshops. She has frequently given her time, traveling long distances on
an inconvenient schedule, to share her commitment to this ministry
of seeking fuller inclusion for others into parish life. For her, the
barrier of feeling excluded from parish activities kept her truly wheelchair bound. But, like the men opening the roof by removing tiles,
Margaret herself began removing the obstacles by volunteering and
found herself in the midst of the work, right where Jesus wanted her
to be.

There are many ways of opening up a roof to let someone down
into the midst of a crowd. Margaret did not have to have her friends

remove tiles from the rafters. But she has found a way in through her response to the parish's search for much-needed workers.

Interacting With Persons Using a Wheelchair

How can you deal comfortably with a person who is in a wheelchair? Here are some tips.

1. Check your home, school, or parish for wheelchair accessibility. Persons may need access even if they are not permanently disabled, but only using a wheelchair because of a temporary condition. Make sure that your doorways are wide enough to accommodate a wheelchair and that aisles are free from obstructions. Provide an entrance ramp so that a wheelchair user can gain access to the building. Also install safety bars and larger door openings in rest rooms.

2. Don't use the person's wheelchair as a place to lean. It is also not a footstool or a stepladder. The chair is considered part of the body space of the person who uses it, and leaning on it is an invasion of that space. Touching or handling someone's wheelchair may be seen as the same as touching or handling the person's body and may be considered inappropriate without the permission of the individual.

3. Maintain eye contact, even if you are standing. Better yet, try to establish eye-level contact by getting a chair and sitting down during the conversation or interaction. Quite often, people who use wheelchairs have to look up at the person who is talking to them. This communicates an unequal status, putting the person in the wheelchair at a disadvantage.

4. However you may be tempted, do not pat someone using a wheelchair on the head. This is condescending behavior.

5. When arranging to meet a person who uses a wheelchair, always give the person advance notice so that time is allowed for arranging transportation. When choosing a place to meet, make

sure there is a ramped or step-free entrance, or elevators, and of course accessible toilet facilities.

6. Do not talk to a person in a wheelchair in a raised volume of speech unless you are specifically asked to do so. A physical disability does not imply a hearing impairment.

7. Ask if assistance is needed, especially if the person needs to use the rest room. The person in the wheelchair can guide you in ways that provide the most effective assistance.

8. In social situations, talk to the person in a wheelchair about topics of interest that you may have in common, such as work, sports, movies, or so on. Do not feel obliged to talk about what it must feel like to use a wheelchair or recount stories of relatives who used a wheelchair. This may make you feel better, but is unlikely to connect well with the person who is in the wheelchair.

Questions for Reflection and Discussion

1. What issues might have to be dealt with for parents if someone like Margaret, or Susan in the previous chapter, were each a teacher in your parish religious education program?

2. What would be the issues for the children?

3. Recall, if you can, instances where people with mobility disabilities were portrayed on TV or in movies. How did these characters figure in the story? Were they portrayed as pitiful or capable? Were they portrayed as independent or dependent.

Challenge

1. Devise a creative approach for including people with disabilities in your parish organizations, committees, and ministries. Share this with your parish council and publish your recommendations for all to see in your weekly parish bulletin.

2. Rent a wheelchair and see how far you are able to navigate in your parish facilities.

3. Reporter John Hockenberry, a paraplegic since an automobile accident when he was nineteen, says this in his memoir *Moving Violations* (New York: Hyperion, 1995):

> *The promise of art and revolution is that people might discard their preconceptions and truly understand what is in the mind of another. What would a world look like in which people dare to wish to know what it is like not to walk?*
>
> JOHN HOCKENBERRY, *MOVING VIOLATIONS: WAR ZONES, WHEELCHAIRS, AND DECLARATIONS OF INDEPENDENCE*

What would this world look like where people are no longer afraid to know what it is like not to walk?

Chapter Five

Sister Monica's Story

Ministry to the Deaf

*Seeing they do not perceive, and hearing
they do not listen!*

MATTHEW 13:13

S ister Monica, whose ministry focuses on helping those who are
deaf, was one of the presenters at our workshop for inclusion.
She follows in the steps of Jesus who made the "deaf to hear," as the
following parable indicates.

*They brought to him a deaf man who had an impediment in
his speech; and they begged him to lay his hand on him. He
took him aside in private, away from the crowd, and put his
fingers into his ears, and he spat and touched his tongue. Then
looking up to heaven, he sighed and said to him, "Ephphatha,"
that is, "Be opened."...Then Jesus ordered them to tell no one;
but the more he ordered them, the more zealously they proclaimed it. They were astounded beyond measure, saying, "He
has done everything well; he even makes the deaf to hear and
the mute to speak."*

MARK 7:32–34, 36–37

I had never met Sister Monica in person before she arrived to
present her first workshop. A nun who was born deaf, she works in
many capacities with deaf individuals in various parishes. Her name

had been given to me by Father Joseph Mulcrone, a priest of the Archdiocese of Chicago who is dedicated to working with the deaf community. He always presides at liturgy using sign language to accommodate deaf people who may be in attendance.

Communication with Sister Monica was intricate. We communicated via a "TTY" setup; that is, a system that allows deaf people to communicate with persons who are not deaf by typing messages. I would contact a relay phone number, and speak with one of the volunteers at the relay office. They would get in touch with her in writing by means of the TTY. She would respond to them in the same way, and they would get back to me. It is a complex but necessary system if communication is to take place.

Since then, I have found that faxes and e-mails are much quicker, and the contact is more satisfactory. Because I am blind, when I receive a printed fax, I must run it through my scanner or wait for someone to read it to me. We went through all this in preparation for Sister Monica's participation in the panel. The time taken was rather substantial, but it proved to be well worth every time-consuming step.

Sister Monica arrived at the Chicago Theological Union quite early. I was greeted by her soft, pleasant voice, "Good morning. I'm Sister Monica." There was no trace of a speech defect, nor any awkwardness that I could detect. I thought, "Perhaps this is the wrong person!" But I ventured a "Good morning and welcome," in reply.

Strange things occur when individuals with different disabilities encounter each other for the first time. We pause (or at least I do), and try to determine the atmosphere of the encounter. "Sister has the advantage over me," I thought, "for she probably knows who I am." But perhaps she didn't. That can often happen. Yet we were soon drinking coffee together, and she was setting up her equipment: an overhead projector, a tape recorder, and a slide projector. She also brought her own interpreter to translate her signed presentation to the workshop participants.

But what happened when she began her talk was quite remarkable. Born deaf, Sister Monica has established her own vocalization patterns. The sounds she uttered while presenting her various slides and transparencies were like a bird warbling—very musical and soft. As she signed her remarks, her interpreter spoke her words aloud to the group.

She told us about variations in sign language in different regions of the country. She had once been taken aback, she said, when signing a lecture in Queens, New York. "They have a different signing dialect in Queens!" she explained. Obviously, that is also true for different dialects spoken by varied ethnic groups. We had never considered that fact before.

As the workshops have continued, other hearing-impaired individuals have been more than willing to volunteer their time and energy to help. They are convinced that the more they spread the positive message of their capabilities, the better it will be for the other half million American Catholics who also have hearing problems. That attitude is shared by all our volunteers. They are anxious to spread the good news to others who might still be unaware of the necessity—and the joy—of opening up the door to inclusion.

What Is Deafness?

Approximately one out of every ten people in your community has a significant hearing loss. Within a population of individuals who are hearing impaired, the overwhelming majority have hearing loss. Only a small number of this group is deaf. Older adults with hearing losses represent over half the total population of people with a hearing loss.

Deafness is defined as a profound inability to hear. It can affect one or both ears. Deafness may be present at birth as a result of a genetic disorder or it may happen later, either suddenly or gradually.

Sometimes a distinction is made between deafness and hearing loss, which does not usually mean completely deaf. It is important to remember that not all hearing-impaired people are 100 percent deaf.

Deafness or hearing loss is usually categorized into two different types. One type is called conductive hearing loss which is caused by anything that blocks the conduction of sound from the outer ear through to the inner ear.

Conductive deafness may be caused by middle-ear infections, blockage of the outer ear (by wax), a collection of fluid in the middle ear, damage to the eardrum by an accident or trauma, and a condition in which the ossicles of the middle ear become unable to move because of the growth of the surrounding bone.

The other type of deafness is called "sensorineural" and refers to damage to the pathway for sound impulses from the hair cells of the inner ear to the auditory nerve and the brain.

The causes for this type of hearing loss include age, loud noises to the hair cells, virus infections of the inner ear (sometimes caused by mumps, measles, or chickenpox), certain drugs, meningitis, strokes, and so on.

People who are deaf or hearing impaired depend on various strategies to communicate: lipreading, hearing aids, aid by interpreters of sign language (a visual language using a combination of hand movements and hand shapes to stand for concepts, letters, and words), finger spelling, alphanumeric pagers, text-messaging devices, e-mail, a TeleTypewriter (TTY) or a Telecommunications Device for the Deaf (TDD), a closed caption decoder to put subtitles at the bottom of the TV screen, vibrating alarm clocks, and so on.

Communicating With People Who Are Deaf

Here is some advice on communicating with people who are disabled through deafness.

1. Ask the deaf person how he or she prefers to communicate, whether it be lipreading, writing, or signing. Patience is a necessary practice for joining a conversation with people who are deaf since it takes longer to communicate.
2. Make sure that there is plenty of light. If you are outside during

the day, make sure that there is some kind of shade to the glare from the sun so it doesn't prevent communication.

3. To get the attention of the person who is deaf, either wave your hand, tap the shoulder gently, flicker the lights, or stomp on the floor if it is a wooden structure and carries vibrations.

4. Do not raise your voice. This strategy seldom works.

5. Adapt your voice and speech patterns. If you normally speak very softly, try to speak louder. If you usually speak rapidly, try to slow down. These adaptations will help both parties in the conversation.

6. Lipreading is still very imperfect. Sometimes only 30 percent of what is being said is transmitted. Thus, try not to change the topic of conversation swiftly and without any transitions. If the person shows signs of being confused, ask if they understood what you said, and repeat your statements if necessary. Check in with the person and ask them if they need something repeated even if they seem to be following along perfectly. Remember that these conversations will take a much longer period of time.

7. Speak at eye level. Do not chew gum, smoke, talk behind a newspaper or with your back to the listener or cover your mouth while you are speaking.

8. Also make sure that there is adequate light so that the movements of your lips and your facial expressions are clearly visible.

9. Make sure that background noises are reduced. Turn off the radio, television, air conditioner, fans, or other noises that might interfere with communication.

10. Come closer so that the listener can see your face more clearly.

11. Be especially aware in group conversations. Be sure to restate the topic every time someone new joins your group. At meetings, it is helpful to put the agenda on a board or overhead, and then indicate the current item under discussion with arrows.

12. Use eye contact and gesture as you wait for a pause in the conversation in order to join in. Then stand by quietly while "overseeing" the discussion until the person you wish to talk to turns to you.

Questions for Reflection and Discussion

1. It is estimated that about 560,000 Catholics in the United States have a hearing impairment. Think about hearing-impaired people you have known in your family, or through other contacts, and share what you have learned from them.
2. What obstacles *do you think* someone with impaired hearing would have if they were doing your job in the parish, and how *do you think* they might overcome those problems?

Challenge

1. Ask a person with a hearing impairment if you are correct in your answer to question #2 above.
2. Download a basic American Sign Language dictionary from the Internet and learn several different words in ASL.
3. The following list of people have hearing loss of one form or another. After each is listed their occupation. Discuss what activities might present a challenge in that person's occupation.

   • Heather Whitestone, winner of the Miss America beauty pageant in 1994
   • Bill Seago, storyteller and actor
   • Ruth Benedict, anthropologist, teacher, and writer
   • Ludwig von Beethoven, music composer
   • Thomas Alva Edison, inventor of the light bulb and the phonograph, and holder of a record number of U.S. patents

4. Comment on the following excerpt from an address by Gregory Hlibok, a deaf attorney in Maryland. He says:

   I have been successful in my life because God guided me through my life. All the decisions in my life are grounded by my faith. My faith formation started in my family life growing up. I grew up in a deaf family. My parents are deaf and I have a sister and a brother. My father went to St. Joseph's school for the deaf, and my mother went to St. Mary's school for the deaf. I was raised Catholic.

Dinnertime was a pleasant experience. When we went to church, there were no interpreters. That was OK because that was a time with God. At dinner was the time when we had discussions about all worldly issues. That was a time when I learned most about my faith.

When it was time for me to receive my first Communion, my parents wanted the priest to accept me, but he refused. My parents fought for me. They found another priest who could sign at another church and he gave me my first Communion.

My obstacles should not have been a barrier to my faith. They shouldn't be for you either. Perhaps your church does not provide interpreter availability and you might use this fact to skip Mass. Don't use that as an excuse not to go to church.

CHAPTER SIX

Bill's Story

A New Spin on Bartimaeus

Domine, ut videam!
LUKE 18:41

Gospel stories about the blind often embarrass and anger blind persons in the pews who squirm through passages in which the blind beg their way through the pages of Scripture.

Here is one instance:

They came to Jericho. As he and his disciples and a large crowd were leaving Jericho, Bartimaeus son of Timaeus, a blind beggar, was sitting by the roadside. When he heard that it was Jesus of Nazareth, he began to shout out and say, "Jesus, son of David, have mercy on me!"

MARK 10:46–47

While the blind Bartimaeus was begging at the side of the road and boldly shouting out, *"Domine, ut videam!"* (Lord, that I may see!), the people around him were trying to shut him up. As a blind person, I would like to shut Bartimaeus up myself whenever this gospel is proclaimed. I want to slide down under the pew and pretend I am not there. I've asked friends who are disabled how they respond to Bartimaeus and his shouting and to the twin blind men stumbling after Jesus. (See Mt 20:29–34.) They all feel as though the congregation has their collective eyes fixed directly on them.

37

In another story of a blind man receiving his sight, this time told in the Gospel of John, Jesus' disciples ask him, "Rabbi, who sinned, this man or his parents, that he was born blind?" People rarely seem to read further in this gospel to understand Jesus' wise reply to his disciples: "Neither this man nor his parents sinned; he was born blind so that God's works might be revealed in him" (Jn 9:3).

So this blind person did indeed reveal God's works; and so have thousands after him. Fading into forgetfulness, however, is that response of Jesus: the purpose of the blind man's disability was to show forth the goodness of God.

In contrast to those gospel personages who beseeched Jesus to cure their blindness, another of our workshop presenters named Bill struggled mightily against his blindness for years.

Bill had been a football player during his university days. A very tall, well-spoken, and well-built man, Bill quickly captured the attention of the participants as he told his story.

Bill had denied the onset of blindness for years. Even after becoming legally blind, he still refused to admit it. Bill surprised the group with his own particular version of this passage from John's gospel. "If I had been around back when Bartimaeus lived," he said, "I would have given that beggar a new white cane and told him to get a job and stop whining. Life is too short to sit around complaining. Get on with it!"

So, how has Bill gotten on with it? At first, he fought against the reality of the fading light. He pretended and bluffed his way through college, holding heavy books up close to his eyes until his head ached. His assignments were turned in later and later as the years went on. He even stayed on the football team and played as rough as the others, hoping he wouldn't overreact and smash into someone unexpectedly.

As an adult, Bill became a Roman Catholic. Yet shortly after his reception into the Church, with the baptismal waters still damp on his forehead, and the light of Christ warm in his heart, he attended a funeral with some business colleagues. Most of them were not Catholic, and none of them were blind. When Communion time arrived, he did not join the congregation in receiving the Eucharist because he did not want anyone from the office to know that he could not see well enough to find his way back to the pew.

Bill went on to tell us that he could never live that lie again. Eventually, he got himself a long white cane, learned how to use it, and at once felt as though he had come out of a dark closet. He accepted his blindness, and realized that the world was already aware of it. The shame of being blind or disabled in any way seems to be deep-seated in our human nature, even among those of us who are disabled. We try to overcome our shame by not acknowledging our impairment. What weight is lifted off our shoulders when we do!

Each day Bill attends Mass before going to work. One morning, a member of the congregation approached him as he silently prayed. She wanted to comfort him by saying that she, too, was praying for his sight to return. Bill assured her that that request wasn't part of his morning prayer and asked her to please stop praying for what he no longer needed.

Sometimes "help" is anything but helpful. Indeed, as in Bill's case, it can be rather offensive. In other situations, it can even be dangerous. People try to avoid dealing directly with disabled individuals, and so they ask anybody standing by—an attendant, a friend, a relative, or a complete stranger—"What is he trying to do?" or "What would she like to drink?" Such behavior is not a courtesy, but relegates the handicapped person to some realm outside ordinary communication.

Human nature is basically good. With God's grace, that goodness is an occasion to see God in others and solicit acts of charity from them. But many people presume they already know what kind of assistance is needed and how it should be given without asking the disabled individual and without understanding what kind of help is appropriate.

Sometimes *not* to offer any help at all is the most helpful thing you can do in particular situations. The easiest resolution, of course, lies in simply asking, "Could I assist you in any way?" Then if the response is positive, "What would you like me to do for you?"

Later, Bill shared that when he could still see well enough, he would usually cross the street to avoid meeting another blind man or woman. He did this because his own sight was not that bad yet, and he wanted nothing to do with the whole blindness thing. However, he also noted, "One of the most important things that has happened to me since then, is Deb, my fiancé. She is blind, and if I had seen her back then when I was in denial, I would have crossed the street just to avoid her. How truly blind can you be. She is the best thing that ever happened to me!"

Bill's behavior paralleled that of the priests and Levites in the parable of the Good Samaritan. They passed by on the other side of the street to avoid helping the wounded traveler.

However, Bill's acceptance of his blindness doesn't necessarily mean that everybody else accepts it. He recounted that as he arrives at the office with his newly acquired white cane, some people still give him a clear signal about how they feel. "Bill, what's with the white cane? You're not blind? You don't look or act blind." The message rang loud and clear. It says, "Keep on pretending that you can see. Then we will find it easier to accept you."

Americans With Disabilities Act (ADA)

Though Bill, in the story just related, was employed at a managerial level, many other folks who are disabled are not economically independent because they lack jobs. This lack of inclusion of people with disabilities in the labor force represents one of the great untapped sources of talented workers in the United States.

Gregory Ellis, director of the Career Center at the nation's largest institution dedicated to the education of the deaf and hard of hearing, says that people with disabilities have the highest instance of unemployment of any group in the country. The passage of the Americans With Disabilities Act (ADA) was meant to remedy that situation and to ensure that a disabled job seeker is not discriminated against in the hiring and the recruiting process.

The ADA also requires employers to make reasonable accommodations for disabled workers—both those who are disabled at the time of hiring and those who become disabled during their time of employment. Many firms report that the cost of accommodating workers who are disabled is much less than they originally estimated.

Myths and Stereotypes

Many people with disabilities are kept from entering the job market because of widespread myths and stereotypes. Here are some typical misconceptions:

1. *A person with mental retardation cannot be trained to perform a job as well as a person without a disability.* False: More than two-thirds of four thousand participants in a Pizza Hut jobs program are people with mental retardation. The current turnover rate among these employees is 20 percent, compared with 150 percent turnover for employees without disabilities. This reduction in turnover translates into a significant drop in training and recruiting costs.
2. *People with disabilities are less productive.* False: People with disabilities work harder on average because they want to ensure their job-related success. They tend to do this because they have something to prove.
3. *A person whose leg has been amputated six inches above the knee cannot load and unload trucks or deliver supplies to various sections of a warehouse.* False: A person with this type of amputation was hired to work in a paper warehouse. He performed the job with no accommodation at all. He worked out so well that the company moved him to a position in which he operated heavy equipment. He was able to climb ladders and use the equipment with no problems.
4. *A person who is blind and is missing his right hand cannot perform a job as a machinist.* False: A man who lost his vision and right hand in Vietnam persuaded a community college to train him as a machinist and was given a job on a trial basis. From his first

day on the job, he broke production records and inspired other workers to do the same. The only accommodation required was moving a lever from the right side of a machine to the left.

One positive result of including those who are disabled in the worshiping community is that it will introduce their talents to a wide variety of potential employers and possibly create a network to communicate job prospects at companies where parish members are already employed.

Questions for Reflection and Discussion

1. As a person without apparent disabilities, what life-situations cause you embarrassment?
2. Why do people tend to look upon people with disabilities as somehow "fragile?"
3. If you were to become disabled—lose your sight or your mobility through an accident or a disease—how would you expect people to treat you differently? Is that the way you treat disabled people when you encounter them now?
4. Have you ever avoided a person with disabilities? How do you feel about that choice now?

Challenge

1. Name and reflect on the disadvantages that *you* have, even as a person who is not classed as disabled.
2. Though Jesus performed miracles in order to confirm his stature as the Son of God, do we need miracles to support our faith? Imagine a different ending to the story of Bartimaeus—one in which Jesus would not restore his sight. What would happen then?

CHAPTER SEVEN

Michael's Story

A Different Kind of Faith Walk

*"And if one blind person guides another, both will fall
into a pit."*

MATTHEW 15:14

*Amazing grace, how sweet the sound
that saved a wretch like me
I once was lost but now am found,
was blind, but now I see.*

TRADITIONAL HYMN

A panelist in one of our earliest workshops was a graduate student in psychology who is now a practicing clinical psychologist. I had been introduced to him by a colleague at the seminary where I was teaching. "If you want to leap into computers," I was told, "you'll have to meet Michael." So we met, and he began to teach me how adaptive computer technology for the blind works.

I followed his instructions, and they were excellent. Afterwards, we kept in contact about the various capabilities of computer technology. We soon began sharing other interests, and I learned more and more about this man and his quest for new areas to conquer. When people who are in some way disabled accept whatever unique situation, problem, grace, or gift they have, only then can they move on and live the rest of their lives.

Michael was constantly searching for other ways to bring the kingdom alive in our midst. He joined various groups working for justice and peace. He was always on the alert for others who might be deeply involved in human rights issues.

One day he chanced upon a group preparing to travel around the world on foot to demonstrate for peace. They would pray along the way and be led by a deeply spiritual Buddhist monk. They planned to set out from a city in Poland in plenty of time to arrive at Hiroshima, Japan, on August 6—the anniversary of the first atomic bomb dropped on that city in 1945. They would then continue on, reaching Nagasaki on August 9, the date on which the next atomic bomb was dropped there.

To support Michael's journey, I made a cash contribution to the group. This financial support was easier to offer than to try to keep up with Michael. I heard from him periodically as the group made its way across Europe and Asia. After his return from this adventure, Michael again joined us as a presenter.

People listened in awed silence as he told about his three-month odyssey, bearing his white cane as a pilgrim's staff and encountering an assortment of responses to his presence with the group. He described specific challenges concerning daily activities like hygiene and sleeping on the ground, in tents, school rooms, or church basements. All his stories were spellbinding.

Occasionally, some super-officious border guards would try to prevent his passage into their countries, not sure what or whom they were encountering. They challenged him with, "How can a blind man make his way without a guide?" Yet Michael always prevailed, sometimes through the intercession of the Buddhist monk. But, if I know Michael, more often than not he took care of it himself.

The most strenuous efforts to stop Michael were experienced as they arrived at the border of India. There he was held up by officials until letters arrived from the United States bearing confirmation from officials sponsoring the Walk for Peace that Michael was indeed a member of the group. Only then did the officials reluctantly watch as he and his cohort continued on their pilgrimage.

But he also told of several villages where the people, alerted to the arrival of these seekers of peace and justice, greeted them with feasts of fine cakes and pure wines as banquets were spread before them. These meals were often prepared by the poor—and sometimes by the not-so-poor—local inhabitants. The pilgrims felt welcomed and invigorated by the hospitality shown, and resumed their trek early the following morning, usually well before the dawn.

In many rural villages in developing countries, many of the officials and teachers are people with disabilities since every person who could work must do so.

The first questions that came from our workshop group were about the purpose of the pilgrimage itself. But soon, after a brief silence, the question everyone wanted to ask came up. "Why would you want to get involved in such a strenuous mission?" He patiently explained that, though he is blind, he doesn't let that prevent him from thinking or feeling, nor from getting involved in important matters. "Since I am a Christian, how can I avoid taking action against what I find wrong? There's too much to do in this world, and I intend to get involved."

Silence followed again, and I had a sense that profound reflections were being generated over the depth of Michael's resolution. People were beginning to see more clearly than they ever had before. "And if the blind lead the sighted," I thought, "they may stay out of the pits and begin their own walk through the world in search of truth and justice—and of peace! Or, perhaps, they will begin to see as God sees, not as human beings see him." (See 1 Sam 16.)

Mobility for Disabled People

The concept of accessibility for those with disabilities is by now an acceptable part of our culture's worthy goals for all our citizens. However, this concept is really much wider than just improving minimum access to jobs, services, and facilities. Instead it should include the idea that everyone has the opportunity to use the full range of transportation services, buildings of whatever kind and purpose, and the open spaces (such as parks and recreational facilities) that make up the places where we all live. When used in this widest sense, and when it also includes the factor of no additional cost for disabled people, this concept needs much more effort in its implementation. Its sense is the inclusion of people with disabilities in all aspects of participation in society.

This concept of mobility should include access to air travel, buildings, buses, educational institutions, ferries, cruise ships, study abroad programs, automobiles, taxis, trains, and walking (for example, unshoveled sidewalks in snowy climates even put people who are not disabled at risk when walking). This means that people with disabilities can go wherever anyone else goes and that they can do so without a lot of difficulty.

Architectural and building concepts include automated doors, lower service counters, elevator controls within reach, alternative furniture at appropriate heights, and preplanned evacuation strategies, among others.

Perhaps an architect familiar with design accessibility for people with disabilities, a travel agent specializing in trip planning for people with limited mobility, or a landscape planner who specializes in accessible outdoor spaces might speak to a group of interested parishioners.

What follows is a brief audit of barriers to worship. This audit is adapted from the book *That All May Worship*, published by the National Organization of Disability, 910 16th Street, NW, Washington, DC 2006; (202) 293-5960. Used with permission.

Attitudinal Barriers

The toughest barriers for people with disabilities to overcome are the attitudes of those who have inadequate information about disability. Reflect about attitudes evident in the worshiping community, and use this list as a springboard for discussion:

- Are persons with disabilities welcome to worship with us? If not, what are we doing wrong?

- Are there members with disabilities that are not apparent?
- Do we recognize the gifts of people with disabilities and are they fully involved in the life of the worshiping community?
- Are people with disabilities given opportunities to serve others within the worshiping community and in outreach programs?
- Are positions of leadership offered to individuals who happen to have a disability?
- How does the worshiping community respond to a religious or lay leader who acquires a serious disability?

Communication Barriers

Communication is the interchange of thoughts, ideas, feelings, and facts. There is a barrier to communication when the content of a message is not understood. Various devices and sensitive actions can help compensate for visual, auditory, or mental disabilities so that every person can absorb the message of God's love.

Use this list to review communication possibilities within the worshiping community. Check the following:

- Services and messages presented verbally and visually.
- Large-print prayer books, hymnals, missals, and Bibles
- Brailled materials
- Homilies or entire services on tape
- Amplifying sound system, in good order
- Sign-language interpreted liturgies, programs
- Adequate lighting
- Real-time captioning
- Audio loops and other assisted listening devices (ALDs)
- Printed homilies and transcription of programs
- An available TDD
- A religious education program that intentionally plans experiences for children, young adults, and older adults with disabilities

- A comfortable way for people with disabilities within the worshiping community to offer suggestions for removing barriers without being made to feel like "whiners" or "complainers."

Architectural Barriers

When beginning to make the architectural and structural changes necessary to welcome people with disabilities, start with things that can be accomplished relatively easily. Get underway! What is needed are visible signs of change, not just never-ending committee meetings and hand wringing.

It is true that aesthetic and historic preservation considerations must be taken into account as worshiping communities make plans to adapt their buildings. And some of these adaptations will be expensive. It is not an acceptable argument, however, to delay because of "how few of them we have." In God's realm, the number of users is not relevant!

Plan a fund-raising strategy that involves everyone, young and old, rich and not-so-rich. Think about everything from bake sales and benefit theatrical presentations to expensive physical changes made in loving memory of some deceased relative.

Begin by consulting members of the worshiping community and their relatives who are architects, contractors, carpenters, and plumbers. Their skills are needed and this is their day to shine. Don't forget to consult, in every phase of evaluation and planning, persons who are users of wheelchairs, walkers, crutches, and canes. By not doing so, many churches and synagogues have made well-intended but inadequate, even wasteful, changes. It goes without saying that all new construction or remodeling should meet current local access codes.

Use this list to review architectural barriers. Check for the following:

Parking and Paths

- Curb cuts to sidewalks and ramps to entrances
- Pathways at least forty-eight inches wide, with a slope of no more than five percent
- Level resting space around doors, five by five feet
- Marked accessible parking spaces close to accessible entrances

Ramps and Stairs

- Ramps thirty-six inches wide minimum, extending one foot in length for every inch of rise, a 1:12 ratio. Thus, a ramp replacing an eight-inch step must extend eight feet.
- Handrails on at least one side of the ramp from rain and snow, which should be protected with nonskid surfaces
- Stairs with handrails on both sides thirty-two inches above the step, and extending a foot beyond the top and bottom of the stairs
- Stairs with rubber treads
- Slightly raised abrasive strips on top steps to warn people with limited sight where stairs begin

Doors and Doorways

- Door openings thirty-two inches wide or more
- Doors which can be opened by exerting five pounds of pressure
- Doors which can be opened electrically by the push of a button
- Lever handles or push bars

Worship Space

- Seating space with extra leg room for people using crutches, walkers, braces, or casts
- Scattered spaces or "pew cuts" for the users of wheelchairs who prefer to be seated in the main body of the worship space, not in the front or back and not in the aisles

- Area with lectern and microphones accessible to those with mobility impairments
- Choir areas allowing wheelchair users to participate
- Adequate lighting directed on the face of any speaker for those who read lips
- Bookstands or lapboards available for those unable to hold prayer books or hymnals

Bathrooms

- At lease one accessible bathroom, ideally one on each floor. These may be unisex, as in an airplane or a home.
- One toilet stall thirty-six inches wide, with forty-eight inches clear depth from door closing to front of commode and a thirty-two-inch door that swings out
- Ideally, a five by five toilet stall with a thirty-two-inch door that swings out and two grab bars, one adjacent to the commode and one behind the commode, to facilitate side transfer from a wheelchair
- A hospital or shower curtain providing privacy for wheelchair users, if metal dividers are removed and other renovations are not possible at the moment
- A sink with twenty-nine inches of clearance from floor to bottom of the sink
- Towel dispensers no higher than forty inches from the floor.
- Lever-type faucet controls and hardware on doors

Water Fountains

- Water fountain mounted with basin no more than thirty-six inches from the floor, easily operated from wheelchairs
- As an interim measure, a supply of paper cups mounted next to the water fountain, or a water cooler

Elevators and Lifts

- Elevator or chair lifts to ensure access to all the major areas of the church

- Controls placed at fifty-four inches or less from the elevator floor, reachable from a wheelchair
- Brailed plaques on elevator control panels
- A handrail on at least one side, thirty-two inches from the floor

Questions for Reflection and Discussion

1. What do you admire most about Michael?
2. What is it that makes people doubt the professional capabilities of someone who has a major disability?
3. If you were a disabled person such as Michael, what travel arrangements would you make in advance to ameliorate the difficulties he encountered?

Challenge

1. Imagine yourself seeking guidance from a practicing clinical psychologist *who is blind*. What questions would you want to ask before beginning your first counseling session? Would you want any *extra assurances* of his or her professional competence before opening your personal life to this person?
2. Look up the story of Jesse and his sons in 1 Samuel, chapter 16, and reflect upon God's choice of someone who seemed to be the least likely candidate for a job.
3. Interview several persons who are disabled to find out their experiences with places and businesses that are signed as "handicapped accessible." What problems do they still encounter? Is the promise of handicapped accessibility always carried through? What can your parish do to remedy any deficits in your area?
4. How would you have handled the situation described in the following story? Comment on the situation as well.

My husband and I [the author], and dog-guide Candide, made plans for a trip to the Stratford Festival in Ontario, Canada, to enjoy the Shakespeare, the talks, and the charming town of Stratford with its excellent restaurants and antique shops. Accommodations had been reserved, tickets purchased, and so we drove north into Ontario from Chicago.

At the door of our picturesque motel—which we had not used on previous trips—we were refused entrance despite our confirmed reservations. "No pets," the angry proprietor snapped.

What to do? Five hundred miles from home, tickets in hand, but nowhere to stay. We took our plight to the Stratford Festival Information Center, and the people there found us a place to stay—for one night only.

In the morning, we started making phone calls. Pilot Dog School in Columbus, Ohio, read Ontario's law to me over the phone while the mayor's office tried to mediate with the obdurate owner of the motel. Nothing doing. Next, the director of the Stratford Tourism Bureau attempted arbitration with the motel owner, but all in vain.

Next, a city attorney was called in. He advised that we could lay a charge before the local magistrate, which we said that we wanted to do. First, we were directed to the local police station to "lay a charge." They were polite but sent us off to a frigidly cold, windowless interrogation room, in the hopes, we suspect, that we would change our minds.

Finally, an officer of the Ontario Provincial Police arrived. He said, "If you really want to press charges, you must be willing to return to Canada to testify when the matter comes before the judge." We replied in the affirmative.

Then he escorted us in his squad car to meet with the suddenly complaisant owners of the motel, who explained that it was all a misunderstanding. If we had only told them what a dog-guide was, and so on and on they went as they attempted to save face.

We moved in for the rest of our stay, accepted an invitation from the City of Stratford to dine at its most exclusive restaurant. The motel owner did not charge us for one night's stay and apologized profusely for the inconvenience he had caused us.

And, we are planning our next trip there this fall, and we plan to stay at the same motel.

CHAPTER EIGHT

Owen's Story

Branching Out

*Ah, but a man's reach should exceed his grasp, or what's
a heaven for?*

ROBERT BROWNING

P eople who attend workshops expect to be offered specific information to assist them in their ministries. They come seeking
supportive, inspirational information, and looking for new ideas or
different ways to invigorate their ministries. They pray, question, share
reflections, and want to leave with a sense that something new has
been discovered that can be incorporated into their work. What they
do not expect is that a presenter will branch out into areas not specifically dealing with their particular ministry, or even appearing
to not deal with "ministry" at all. People come simply seeking how to
accommodate parishioners who have limitations that make it difficult or impossible to be involved in ordinary church activities.

But one presenter, Owen, surprised the workshop participants
by offering a far broader consideration. He quickly turned the participants' attention from mere acceptance of people with disabilities
to the wide world of advocacy for crucial changes in society.

He quoted the unacceptable numbers of qualified individuals
with disabilities who are unemployed or underemployed—more than
70 percent. He spoke of the depression—mental, physical, and
moral—that exists among populations to whom all doors seem
closed, or only slightly open for the exceptional few to enter. He also

addressed the utmost necessity of changing social structures by changing laws and by confronting society with the challenge to open opportunities for training that will enable eager individuals with disabilities to qualify as productive participants in society.

Owen pointed to leaders with disabilities who are now emerging to change the stereotype of disability—successful lawyers, teachers, artists, parents, and students. As a leader in the National Federation of the Blind (NFB), he spoke enthusiastically about this, the largest of several organizations energetically engaged in advocacy for the blind. The NFB works and struggles in the secular and political community to achieve life, liberty, equality, and full employment for those it represents. It gathers people with visual disabilities to advocate effectively before local, state, and federal authorities on issues concerning the blind. And there are many similar organizations for individuals with different specific disabilities, all striving to change society's attitudes and the limitations that prevent many from living full and productive lives in our world.

Some participants wondered, "What has this to do with our purpose here today?" But why should advocacy *not* be part of our efforts for inclusion within parish communities? These people are fellow parishioners, neighbors, friends, relatives, and even ourselves who must be included in the "so-called" normal population, as well as in our faith communities. We may try to divide life into separate compartments, but if our worship on Sunday (or whatever day you keep holy), is lived separately from the rest of the week, we have obviously not achieved a full understanding of true inclusion, nor of the gospel.

Psychologists warn that individuals who persistently feel subjected to negative attitudes will eventually succumb to a fatal hypnotic state and simply give up. Some live in quiet desperation and yield to the monotony of their fate as second-class citizens, or as "do-nothing" human beings.

John Donne, the metaphysical poet, speaks of the despair of those who feel so neglected:

Though thou with clouds of anger do disguise
Thy face; yet through that mask I know those eyes,
Which, though they turn away sometimes,
Never will despise.

But the Holy Spirit's winds of change are blowing through our world. In recent years, religious and civic leaders have started to become aware of the mounting problems faced by the disenfranchised. They are seeking programs to rectify that appalling situation. Thus, in 1980, the United Nations declared a decade of concern for individuals with disabilities. And by the time the U.S. bishops issued their *Pastoral Statement of the U.S. Catholic Bishops on People With Disabilities* in 1978, the problem had already been addressed by others. To their credit the American bishops had noted the following in paragraph 6 of their document:

In a spirit of humble candor, we must acknowledge that at times we have responded to the needs of some of our people with disabilities only after circumstances or public opinion have compelled us to do so.

They confess that the secular world has led the way toward improving the sorry lot of disabled individuals through laws and ordinances. The Church has often heeded the signs of the times as a Johnny-come-lately. Yet, the bishops clearly recognize that the Church must continue to offer aid and service to the disabled, and it must never forget that providing such support is itself a privilege. "When we extend our healing hands to others," the bishops declare in paragraph 6 of their statement, "We are healed ourselves."

But the most important aspect of this historic public statement is that it specifically sets out to bring the disabled within the purview of John XXIII's vision as expressed in his encyclical *Mater Et Magistra*. To this end, the bishops, in paragraph 1 of their statement, have issued this summons:

[We] call upon people of good will to reexamine their attitudes toward their brothers and sisters with disabilities and promote their well being, acting with the sense of justice and the compassion that the Lord so clearly desires.

Other voices have been heard. James Shapiro, in his book *No Pity: People With Disabilities Forging a New Civil Rights Movement* (New York: Times Books, 1994), provides appalling statistics on the low cost of mainstreaming disabled people in comparison to the very high cost of warehousing them in custodial institutions. It would be far more economical, as well as more humane (even more, Christian!) to train, educate, and assist people to achieve independent status rather than putting them out of our sight in nursing homes or mental hospitals.

No survey has been taken to tally the wasted lives of people who could be productive, useful citizens, and creative contributors to society. Might some of these be among those we wish to include in our parish activities? Or do we also quietly avoid inviting into the fold these unfortunate dropouts who can be difficult to assimilate?

Prophets in the Hebrew Scriptures and the whole New Testament proclaim a new covenant:

But this is the covenant that I will make with the house of Israel after those days, says the LORD. I will put my law within them, and I will write it on their hearts; and I will be their God, and they shall be my people (Jer 31:33).

How can we help the less-abled people in our society to come to know, with the poet, that God does not turn away from them, and will never despise them.

It is hard to avoid the prevailing negative attitude which many people in both secular and religious society still hold toward people with disabilities. It clearly behooves us to realize that many individuals, seeking to gain equal opportunity and full status, have formed advocacy organizations to change laws—and to change attitudes—

with considerable success in this modern era that focuses on human rights and dignity. But the work is far from complete.

Faith That Reaches Out

Long before the federal government began talking about "faith-based initiatives," churches across the country have been committed to social outreach work that assists those who are disabled. Here are a few examples.

Grace Episcopal Church in White Plains, New York, sponsors a neighbor-to-neighbor program that provides home care to help those who are disabled and who are elderly. A staff of personal care aides, home health aides, and nurses, through contracts with local health care agencies, delivers medical care; the help also includes house cleaning, cooking, and grocery shopping.

Emmanuel Episcopal Church in Delaplane, Virginia, operates a day care for disabled children. Mary's Family, which opened in the parish hall, serves a county that has some fourteen hundred families with disabled children. Named for founder Martha Toomey's grandmother, the day care will be open one Saturday a month.

An example of the kind of children who attend includes a twelve-year-old boy with Down syndrome and autism who behaves erratically, requiring his parents' constant attention. While there, children are cared for by volunteers—adults as well as children—and a registered nurse.

Our Lady of Mercy Catholic Church in Potomac, Maryland, started an organization called Best Buddies that seeks to enhance the lives of people with mental retardation by providing opportunities for one-to-one friendships and integrated employment. The group got its start after parishioners turned to their pastor for help in caring for their severely disabled daughter. The organization originally was planned to provide respite care, but it has expanded to offer activities such as sports, photography, music, and weekly chat sessions for young men and women that deal with teen issues such as dating and becoming independent. A group of volunteers from community organizations, such as the camera club, the garden club, and local sports teams, help run activity programs and assist members.

McLean Bible Church, located near Tysons Corner, offers two special-needs Bible classes each Sunday morning. Called the Beautiful Blessing Children's Ministry, the classes are designed for children who need one-to-one attention or who are medically fragile. Most Sundays, six to eight children with various mental and physical disabilities attend each class while their parents attend worship services. Volunteer nurses assist the most severely disabled, including several children who receive nourishment through feeding tubes and one child who is deaf and blind and has a seizure disorder.

Questions for
Reflection and Discussion

1. Inventory the worshiping communities in your area to see how far each has gone in providing accessible premises and services.
2. What experiences will help people in your parish form more positive attitudes toward people with disabilities?
3. What specific steps can your parish or church membership take to help those who are disabled, not only to become full members of your worshiping community, but also to assist them to because full citizens in secular matters as well?

   At a special forum, present this plan to your pastor and parishioners for implementation.
4. Discuss aspects of this story that follows:

   Most people are aware that it is the responsibility of a citizen to serve on juries when a summons is issued. However, when someone who is disabled receives a summons for jury duty, the usual response is to call up the clerk of the court, state the disability involved, and be released from service.

   However, when I receive a summons for jury duty, I went downtown with my dog-guide to answer the summons. When

I arrived, an armed bailiff stopped me and explained, "Miss. There has been a mistake. You don't have to serve," as he firmly tried to ease me out the door.

"No, no," I replied. "I want to serve. I am very anxious to serve!" The bailiff's response was a look of incredulous amazement. I firmly moved to the elevator and pushed the button to arrive at the seventeenth floor.

I presented my summons, and the officials on the other side of the table consulted with each other. One said, "Well, if she insists, what can we do?" The other had a good idea: "Give her the badge with the number one so she will have an easy time remembering her number when it is called. After all, she can't see!"

So the first hurdle had been cleared, not without its erroneous assumptions, though now I was free to make my way into what was called "the bull pen." There the prospective jurors milled about, exchanging names. I met a neighbor, and we began to chat.

When the call came for jurors, officials would spin a large drumlike container and draw out the numbers of the jurors to be assigned to each jury pool. Finally, my number was called, and I was taken by a deputy to a courtroom on another floor. Here the lawyers interrogate prospective jurors to decide if they were to be selected to actually serve on a jury.

My turn came, and a prosecutor asked me pointed questions about how someone who could not see would be able to make a reasonable judgment over certain types of evidence. I explained that, as a college professor, I dealt with printed material all the time and had several means of evaluating such materials.

Even the judge joined in the questioning and concluded that he found my capabilities adequate to the tasks at hand. I was thrilled.

But just as I began to breathe easily, one of the attorneys for the defense returned for additional questions. Sensing the *inevitable, and before he had finished complimenting me on my degrees and fine education, I gathered up my belongings and stepped down from the jury box.*

Several of the other jurors seemed to be disturbed. One of them spoke up and asked to be removed as well. Another joined in and asked to be excused too. The judge soon calmed the situation down, and those who had not been selected were ushered out of the court room.

Later that day, as I wandered out into Daley Plaza for lunch, I overheard a policeman assigned to watching the city Christmas tree being decorated say to someone as I passed by, "There goes the blind woman who was dismissed by the lawyer for General Motors. I think that might have been poor judgment on his part."

At the end of our two weeks, we were informed by the bailiff that anyone who wanted to know about the decision on any specific case had the right to call back and ask when the case was over.

Of course, I did, and learned that General Motors had lost.

Preferred Guidelines for Referring to Those With Disabilities

As the story about jury duty for someone who is blind illustrates, society holds many negative assumptions and misconceptions about those who are disabled. These assumptions may not seem important to the person without apparent disabilities, but these misconceptions can be perpetuated not only by actions but also by language that may cause unnecessary offense to people who are disabled. Depending on how it is used, language can reinforce either a positive or a negative view of a person with disabilities. Here is a guide to some preferred usages, but remember it is the context of the statement that can often create hidden meanings. And, since language changes, these can only be tentative guidelines. Each geographical area or special social group may have other preferred usages.

In general, the preferred language always describes people who are disabled in an active rather than a passive role. For example, "wheelchair bound" portrays a negative image of a person, while "wheelchair user" is an active term that shifts the emphasis from the wheelchair to the person. Another example is the use of the word "special" when referring to a person who is disabled. This word tends to mean "not good enough" or "extraordinary," and therefore may be viewed as patronizing or condescending.

Sometimes use of words meant to avoid the reality of a person's disability can be seen as over-compensation and uninformative. "Differently-abled," "physically challenged," and "inconvenienced" are often seen as labels of this type.

Another attitudinal misperception is often couched in the well-meaning but condescending comments, such as "Isn't it wonderful how he has conquered his disability?" People who live with disabilities want to be accepted for who they are, not as out-of-the-ordinary and rare "heros."

Also keep in mind that the use of the terms "nondisabled" or "persons without disabilities" is preferable to the term "normal" when comparing persons with disabilities to others. Use of the word "normal" makes the unspoken comparison of "abnormal," thus stigmatizing those individuals with differences.

Here is a guide to terms used for people with disabilities. On one side is the word or phrase that may perpetuate misperceptions of others; on the other side is a term that is considered preferable. These represent only a selected list and they are intended as suggestions only.

NONPREFERRED LANGUAGE		PREFERRED LANGUAGE
Disabled	*Sees person only in terms of disability*	Use "people with disabilities"
Mentally retarded	*Generalizes that all people in this category are alike, does not see as people as individuals*	Use "persons with mental retardation"
Deaf, blind	*Categorizes people by their defect instead of their humanity*	Use "deaf people," "blind citizens"
Handicapped	*Use of "handicapped" vs. "Disabled" vs. "Impaired" is still being debated*	Use these terms with care
Invalid	*Faulty usage since many with disabilities are not ill*	Do not use
Abnormal	*People with disabilities seen as "less than"*	Do not use
Defective (birth)	*Objectifies/dehumanizes person*	Use "person with congenital disability"

NONPREFERRED LANGUAGE		PREFERRED LANGUAGE
Dan is afflicted with, stricken with, or suffers from polio; Dole is an arthritic patient.	*Labels deny other aspects of person; objectifies person as mere object of medical care; implies dependency, defeat*	Give facts: "Dan had polio. Dole has arthritis."
Victim: Sam was a polio victim.	*Implies pity and lack of ability*	Do not varnish facts: "Sam had polio."
Deaf and dumb, dummy, deaf-mute	*Connotes that person with physical disability also is mentally incapacitated*	Use "deaf," "hearing-impaired," "speech-impaired"
Sightless, blind as a bat, four eyes	*Discourteous*	Use "blind," "partially sighted," "vision impaired"
Deformed, hunchbacked, maimed	*Implies repulsion, circus-like deformity, discourteous*	Use "has spinal curvature," "has a physical disability"
Confined to a wheelchair, wheelchair-bound	*Creates erroneous impression that people in wheelchairs never leave this apparatus to sit in chairs, drive cars, and so on*	Use "wheelchair user," "uses a wheelchair," "wheelchair using"

NONPREFERRED LANGUAGE		PREFERRED LANGUAGE
Nut, maniac, insane, crazy, mentally ill, psycho	*Slang terms that are no longer accepted, demeaning, and creates stigmatization*	Use "behavior disorder," "emotional disability," "mental disability"
Retard, slow, simple-minded, Mongoloid, idiot	*Humiliating and shaming*	Use "people with mental retardation"
Monster, vegetable, freak	*Makes people with severe disabilities into mythical oddities, inhumane*	Use "This person has multiple or severe disabilities."
Hank is epileptic, Jane is brain-damaged, Liz is arthritic.	*These references make people into their disabilities and reduces them to only one aspect of their life.*	Use "Hank has epilepsy," "Jane has cerebral palsy," "Liz has arthritis."
Cripple, crip (an "insider" word), crippled	*These usages are demeaning and offensive.*	John had a physical disability.
Moron, feeble-minded, imbecile	*Outdated medical terminology reflecting social beliefs rather than medical language*	Do not use

We must educate ourselves to rid our language of the "tragedy" of "birth defects," "victims" of diseases "struggling" to remake their lives. As we do this, we should keep in mind Mark Twain's advice: "The difference between the right word and the almost right word is the difference between lightning and the lightning bug."

Questions for Reflection and Discussion

1. Discuss the meaning of this Chinese proverb in the light of language used to refer to those who have disabilities: "The beginning of wisdom is to call things by their right name."
2. Discuss the difference between "mere inclusion" and "public advocacy" for people with disabilities. How can you as an individual be an advocate for persons with disabilities?

Challenge

1. Name areas of ministry or volunteer options in your parish that would provide people with disabilities opportunities for full participation.
2. Make an inventory of the liturgies and sacraments in your diocese that are available to people with disabilities, for example, the sacrament of reconciliation for the deaf, interpreted Masses for the hearing impaired, or even bingo for the blind. Attend one of these liturgies or events and report back to your planning group.

CHAPTER NINE

Elizabeth's Story

The Hierarchy of Disabilities

*Then the LORD said to Cain, "Where is your
brother Abel?" He said, "I do not know; am I
my brother's keeper?"*

GENESIS 4:9

*For just as the body is one and has many members,
and all the members of the body, though many, are one
body, so it is with Christ....On the contrary, the members of the body that seem to be weaker are indispens-
able, and those members of the body that we think are
less honorable we clothe with greater honor.*

1 CORINTHIANS 12:12, 22–23

S aint Paul, writing those words about the Mystical Body of Christ
almost two thousand years ago, was obviously celebrating the
mutuality of the Christian experience and its bond to Christ. The
body is one, and each member has an important function within the
whole. He tells us that the eye is not better than the foot or the hand,
but simply different.

At the same time, Paul was alluding to some physical impairment in his own body, perhaps of his vision, since he was struck
blind as he was on his way to Damascus. (See Acts 9:3–9.)

And, again in the Epistle to the Galatians, Paul speaks of illness:

"You know that it was because of a physical infirmity that I first announced the gospel to you; though my condition put you to the test, you did not scorn or despise me, but welcomed me as an angel of God, as Christ Jesus... .Had it been possible, you would have torn out your eyes and given them to me."

GALATIANS 4:13–15

And, most notably in 2 Corinthians, Paul says:

"Therefore, to keep me from being too elated, a thorn was given me in the flesh....Three times I appealed to the Lord about this,...but he said to me, 'My grace is sufficient for you, for power is made perfect in weakness'" (2 Cor 12:7–9).

In modern-day experience, we are prone to setting up our own patterns of discrimination between one person and another, including one that involves a hierarchy, or perhaps we should say a "lower-archy," within the handicapped community. Some might find such a pattern of discrimination curious. Why would people with one disability wish to lord it over others with a different disability? The answer is simple: human nature is weak. We feel less vulnerable, even less disabled, if we can look down on someone else we consider more impaired than we are.

People who are blind may be perceived to be at a greater disadvantage than people who can see, who can read, or who can enjoy works of art and the beauty of nature with its magnificent colors. Yet, for someone who is blind, the glories of music, singing birds, and conversations with a friend are life giving and cherished. Blind persons depend almost entirely on their imaginations, or if they were not born blind, on memory. On the other hand, someone who is hearing impaired, or totally deaf, may look like a normal person. They can drive a car, read, travel, and go on with daily life minus the annoyance of chaotic sounds, overhead jets, roaring cars and buses, the boom of fireworks, and so on.

But times are changing. Aware of the movement toward human

rights, Congress passed the Rehabilitation Act of 1973. This law prohibits discrimination against individuals with disabilities in any federally funded institution throughout the country. This important piece of legislation has begun to bring changes in our society, but it will require the ongoing cooperation of us all to achieve full implementation.

It was under this law that I was hired to work in an office serving students with disabilities at Citywide Colleges in Chicago. That unusual environment is staffed almost entirely by persons with disabilities. Employees with varying types of disabilities were all clustered together in one location. There I had the opportunity to witness an intense in-house hierarchy. The insights I gained are essential for anyone dedicated to working in ministries for or with people who have disabilities. How, for example, does someone confined to a wheelchair communicate on an equal basis (or should I say equal footing), with someone who is blind? I learned much while working there, and I had much to contemplate afterwards.

Each disability has its own special needs; for example, a blind person entering a room does not know who is present without someone identifying who is there. That is the same courtesy one expects when answering a telephone: to be informed whom he or she is talking to.

So, as I arrived at my new job in this office, I expected to be introduced to the other individuals and to be given a tour to become familiar with the new environment. Since that was overlooked, I resorted to my own methods of discovery: listening in on conversations and remaining alert to sounds and noises around me, imagining from whence they came. Soon the office became populated with fellow employees, and I began to learn—by listening—what disability each had, where they sat, and what their jobs were.

I discovered that, not far from my desk, Donna, one of the secretaries, was receiving assistance to get situated at her typewriter because alone she was incapable of lifting her partially paralyzed arms. Once in position, she was an excellent typist.

One morning, I set about assembling the coffee pot before getting down to work. When Donna wheeled herself in to the office, she asked if I would mind helping her get her coat off. In turn, I asked her where the coffee pot was. That's how we began to get to know each other. When we each finished our tasks, Donna offered to "walk over" to my desk so we could make luncheon plans. She also informed me of the location of certain books I needed to scan in order to make my talking computer read text aloud to me. It was through helping each other that the wall of strangeness began to crumble.

One day, Donna wanted to go to Marshall Field's, a major Chicago department store, to buy her sister a birthday present, a blouse, and we decided to go together. Shopping at Marshall Field's has always been a delight for me, so I eagerly wanted to accompany her. What a journey we had! Donna, in her electric-powered chair, wheeled, or "walked," as she would say, along the gutter to avoid curbs, and I walked on the sidewalk next to her. The busy downtown street with its noisy traffic roared along at our side. People looked at us. Whenever we needed help with doors, a nice man or woman would emerge from among the onlookers and open it for us.

Inside Marshall Field's, we encountered our next obstacles. The blouses were hung on rods too high for Donna to reach. So, as she picked out ones she liked, I handed them to her to check the size and price. In that way, we covered for each other's disability, and there are always the spectators, pretending to be going about their own business, who were usually near enough to offer information when we needed assistance.

Then we sought out the music department, discovering that it was down a flight of stairs, inaccessible by wheelchair. Steps are no problem for someone who cannot see, but reading labels is. I walked down the stairs, returning to show Donna the labels of recordings she might want to buy. Then, back down I went to purchase those she chose. Together we had worked out a system enabling us to respond to each other's needs.

Back in the office, I continued listening to my new surroundings. Soon I learned about those who occupied nearby desks. I could often hear the soft Hispanic voice of Jaime, who usually was giving advice and counsel to people over the telephone. His manner was so gentle that I felt compelled to listen. I wanted to meet this kind-sounding young man. But I noticed that people coming to the office tended to go around his desk, then pause at mine, to ask questions. I wondered why. Later I learned that although his voice was soothing, and his countenance handsome and well-proportioned with fine Hispanic features, Jaime was a "thalidomide offspring," with a truncated body and only vestigial arms and legs.

People without disabilities seemed to have no problem talking to me, in or out of the office, because, as I have been told, they could easily overlook the fact that I cannot see. "I forget you are blind," they patronizingly say. "You don't look blind at all." But it was impossible to overlook Jaime's appearance or Donna's pronounced physical limitations. But I had no problem with them—what I can't see doesn't cause me to judge others. What a blessing God has given me!

Surveys and questionnaires indicate that of all the varieties of disabilities, blindness has the honor of occupying the lowest status. I was once asked to moderate a discussion at a business meeting for people who wished to learn how to hire individuals with disabilities. Each participant responded to a survey intended to determine which disabilities would be most difficult for them, as potential employers, to accept, and what disability would be most unproductive, or most difficult, to fit into their work scheme. In every case, blindness had the dubious honor of being seen as the least desirable disability of all.

As a blind person that amazes me. I have always cherished my independence, and I have a hard time imagining how people confined to a wheelchair deal with the embarrassment of needing intimate personal care from others. That would be most difficult for me. I love music and the sounds of birds. I love concerts, operas, drama, and singing. Not being able to hear the beauty of Handel's *Messiah* or Menotti's *Amahl and the Night Visitors,* the many Christmas carols and church bells, and the affectionate whimpering of my golden retriever would be a hardship, indeed.

However, I have had to accept the results of this survey despite my personal disgruntlement over it, for I have learned that its conclusions can be substantiated. Its validity came home to me with resounding clarity when I encountered a man asking for money on the sidewalk outside the office where I worked. Homeless people wandering the streets are avoided by most of us who prefer to pass by "on the other side of the road." People were scurrying past him, but his voice kept crying out. When the footsteps came near me, reaching out, I offered him a dollar. He hesitated; I waited, dollar in hand. Then, he said, "No thanks, lady. I'm not that bad off yet," obviously referring to my blindness. He left me standing, dollar bill in hand, face reddening.

In refusing my dollar, even this man on the street identified himself with those who had taken the survey. Those business people used the survey's results to hire or not hire prospective applicants. I wondered if that street person, too, would be refused a job were he to apply for one of their openings.

The hierarchy of disabilities has existed even as far back as the Book of Leviticus (21:17) which prohibits anyone with a disability from offering sacrifice to God under pain of excommunication:

No one of your offspring throughout their generations who has a blemish may approach to offer the food of his God.

In that ancient society, certain restrictions were enforced to prevent spreading illnesses. However, this proscription speaks not to a disease, but to a disability.

Another experience occurred one rainy evening as I waited with my well-trained guide-dog for a taxi I had called. The driver had confirmed my phone call and I was eager to get home. I stood at the curb so I would be ready when he pulled up. The taxi slowed down, but as it neared the curb the driver called out that he couldn't take me with the dog because it was Ramadan, and dogs are considered unclean.

I stood there, not sure what to do, as another taxi pulled up and the driver encouraged me get in before I got wetter. I thanked him, and as I entered the cab with my dog he explained that he liked doing nice things for people because it was the time of Ramadan, and he considered my presence an opportunity to do good. So, I asked, "What's the difference between you and the taxi that refused my business?" "He's just wrong and I'm right," he laughingly answered. I wanted to explain that I was grateful he stopped, although according to the law he is required to accept my business, and that's true for all providers of public accommodation and transportation.

Once I asked my husband, who is not blind, which would he prefer: blindness, deafness, or an inability to walk. His response surprised me. After all, I had raised five children, kept our home clean, cooked meals, obtained my degree, went to concerts and plays without concern for stairs or architectural barriers. In short, I could do and enjoy almost everything but driving a car. In addition, nowadays recordings of all kinds of literature are available on cassettes and disks, computers and scanners are available that can give voice to what is on the printed page, all allowing individuals who cannot see access to printed material formerly out of their range.

But my husband replied, "Deafness." His answer was reasonable. He is aware of the difficulty of receiving a good education without being able to hear lectures and of maintaining relationships without conversation. Yet, if he were to choose a disability later in life, after he had grown up and was educated, he thought deafness would be easiest for him to adjust to.

Do you recall the old anecdote about the celestial warehouse where each person can select his or her own cross to bear? They could trade in the one they had been given for whichever one they found most comfortable. Unfortunately, life does not work like that! The familiar story concludes with its fine moral: when the various crosses had been tried on for size, the searcher inevitably exits the heavenly warehouse with the cross he came in with, ready to resume the place on his or her own particular *via dolorosa!*

Questions for
Reflection and Discussion

1. What could you learn from a person who is blind? What could you learn from a person who lives in a wheelchair?
2. How do you treat differently people with various different disabilities? Why do you do so?
3. Which disability would you pick now and later in life if offered the opportunity? Share with your group the reasons for your choice.
4. As recently as the 1960s, some U.S. municipalities passed statutes known as "ugly laws," which stated that the sight of people with disabilities was offensive. Such laws proclaimed that "no person who is diseased, maimed, mutilated, or in any way deformed, so as to be an unsightly or disgusting object, is to be allowed in or on the public ways or public places." How do these laws fit in with the American ideal of youth and physical beauty? How long might the effect of such laws be felt even if they were repealed? Do places still have these "laws" on the books, even if unwritten?
5. Research the "eugenics" codes of the Nazi government in pre-World War II Germany. How did they handle the "problem" they perceived with people with disabilities, those with mental illness, and those who did not fit the image of the blond, Aryan German?
6. How does the current craze with plastic surgery—liposuction, face lifts, tummy tucks, gastric bypass operations, and nose jobs—show our attitude to the "non-perfect" body?

Challenge

1. Examine your own attitudes and how you may "look down upon" people (1) who are blind; (2) who are deaf; or (3) who are in a wheelchair.
2. Think about those times that you have used religion as an excuse to not get involved in helping someone who needed you. Confess these to a priest, minister, or to some close friend.

CHAPTER TEN

Laurie's Story

Definitions of Disability

It is better to feel compunction than to define it!
THOMAS À KEMPIS, *THE IMITATION OF CHRIST*

A man was there named Zacchaeus; he was a chief tax collector and was rich. He was trying to see who Jesus was, but on account of the crowd he could not, because he was short in stature. So he ran ahead and climbed a sycamore tree to see him, because he was going to pass that way. When Jesus came to the place, he looked up and said to him, "Zacchaeus, hurry and come down; for I must stay at your house today."

LUKE 19:2–5

Apparently, Zacchaeus was very short, or as we would say today, he was "vertically challenged." Should Zacchaeus be considered disabled? Usually, when we think of people with disabilities, we conjure up the trio of the blind, the deaf and the lame. However, many other physical, emotional, and mental problems need to be listed under the general definition of "disability."

The *Random House Dictionary* defines disability as "any disorder that makes success more difficult," and as "a physical or mental disorder, especially one that makes ordinary activities of daily living difficult." Thus, our traditional concept of a disability must expand, especially as the human population advances in age. Over one-third of those with disabilities became so after age fifty-five, mainly through degenerative or debilitating illnesses.

The ancient philosopher, Aristotle, proposed a definition of the human being which also helps determine what constitutes a disability. For him, "disability" comes under the category of a characteristic or a quality—in philosophical terms, an "accident"—such as color, height, and weight that does not compromise the definition of an individual's human essence.

Human beings are composed of body and soul, which is their essence, and they have many characteristics that are not essential to the nature of being human, but are, philosophically speaking, merely "accidental" to that particular individual. What is essential is that we all belong to the species "rational animal." Other characteristics, while important, do not take away or add to the basic essence of the human being as a human being.

If, for example, one were to lose a foot or an arm, or if one's hair turned gray, those things do not take away from the essence of being a human being. Therefore, any individual with a disability must still be categorized as a human being. People with disabilities are not second-class citizens, and certainly not second-class Christians. Some primitive cultures consider a person without sight as having no soul, and thus belonging to a different species. On the other hand, we can look to the respect given to the blind seer, Tiresias (the blind Theban seer who figures in Greek mythology) and to the blind poet, Homer, in ancient literature.

Thus, we find in the dictionary, in Aristotle, and in literature varied perspectives on physical limitations. So who falls outside our perception of what is "normal," or what are usual human characteristics? Two students of mine have taught me much about size disability.

People who are abnormally short might be referred to as "midgets," or "dwarfs." The medical terms describing the reasons for their situation vary widely, but what is clear is that the physical and social barriers these individuals face are enormous. Their stature does not allow them easy mobility in our world of curbs, stairs, countertops, and other architectural barriers. The standard automobile, musical instrument, and even blue jeans assume proportions totally out of their range.

Laurie called herself "a little person." Genetic dwarves encounter many obstacles that compare easily with the constraints faced by the blind, deaf, and lame. While walking along regular streets, Laurie says bushes become like trees, and someone's dog assumes the stature of a horse. She writes music but it is hard to find a guitar small enough for her to play.

She is always aware of people staring at her, giving the impression that they consider her a freak. One cold winter afternoon, she hurried across an enormous downtown street with huge tires spinning past her at shoulder height. A traffic officer called out, "Where are you going? Isn't the circus in session during the holidays?"

In nonthreatening situations Laurie usually maintains a good sense of humor. While diagraming sentences at the blackboard, I asked her to insert commas at the proper places. As she approached the looming blackboard, reaching up on tiptoe for chalk, she commented, "If I keep jumping, I'm sure to hit the right spot sooner or later."

The definition of a disability has changed for me as I have become aware of the obstacles many people endure. Many challenges confront individuals of abnormal weight or height. I once taught literature and philosophy at a local college seminary. Through the years, I became friends with Thomas, a student enrolled in my classes. We often talked about his dreams for the future and his hopes to serve among the poor after ordination.

Thomas had a beautiful tenor voice and he was selected to sing the Martyrology for the seminary's Advent liturgy during his senior year. My husband joined me in the chapel that snowy December night. "That's Tom," I whispered. "Remember? I told you about his lovely voice?"

"That's Tom?" my husband whispered back. He sounded a bit surprised. In the car after the festivities, he remarked, "Did anyone ever tell you about Tom's appearance?" I asked, "What do you mean?"

"He is a very large fellow," he said. "Perhaps enormous would be a better word. I wonder how he gets along with the other students. They all seem so serious about their looks—jogging, running, and all that routine. Young men today are very aware of the impression they make on people. You know, we live in an age of fitness."

People of unusual size, either large or small, have problems that can be difficult to live with or accommodate. Others make judgments just by sight that can close doors to them. Perhaps, the definition of a disability must assume a far greater dimension than we at first thought.

Questions for Reflection and Discussion

1. As a group, what limitations should be given official disability status. Are there other conditions you would add?
2. Should a newly arrived immigrant, who does not yet speak English, be considered disabled in our American culture? Why or why not?
3. Discuss the implications of the quote that follows from Rosemarie Garland Thomson's book *Extraordinary Bodies* (New York: Columbia University Press, 1996):

Disability is a system that produces subjects by differentiating and marking bodies. Furthermore, this comparison of bodies legitimates the distribution of resources, status, and power within a biased social and architectural environment. The category of disability exists as a way to exclude the kinds of bodily forms, functions, impairments, changes, or ambiguities that call into question our cultural fantasy of the body as a neutral, compliant instrument of some transcendent will. Disability is a broad term, within which cluster ideological categories as varied as sick, deformed, ugly, old, maimed, afflicted, abnormal, or debilitated—all of which disadvantage people by devaluing bodies that do not conform to cultural standards. Thus, disability functions to preserve and validate such privileged designations as beautiful, healthy, normal, fit, competent, intelligent—all of which provide cultural capital to those who can claim such status."

4. Read this story (from *How It Feels to Live With a Physical Disability* by Jill Krementz, New York: Simon & Schuster, 1992) about an eight-year-old who is a dwarf. How would you have dealt with this situation?

Mommy calls me a short-statured person, but I usually call myself a short person because it's easier. Some people think I'm a midget but that's because they don't know the difference between a dwarf and a midget. A midget is a miniature person. Everything's smaller than average—head, body, and arms and legs. A dwarf has a normal-sized head and body, but has short arms and legs. Lots of dwarfs are bowlegged, and the reason for this is that our small legs get bowed from carrying so much weight....

Even though most people do know something about dwarfs, they still stare whenever I go to the beach. I can see them looking at me....I guess the hardest part about being a short-statured person is that most people don't know much about us. They've read Snow White and the Seven Dwarfs and in that story the dwarfs are treated like little simpletons. That's not how we are. Our brains are fine!

5. Comment on the results of a recent study that indicated that short-statured people make less money on average than those who are taller. Would you expect this to be true?

Challenge

1. Make a list of the struggles people might experience who (1) are severely overweight; (2) have arthritis; (3) have narrow peripheral vision; (4) are color blind; (5) have a chronic disease such as

diabetes, HIV/AIDS, or heart disease; (6) suffer from bi-polar disease or manic depression; (7) are claustrophobic, have a fear of heights, or a fear of crowds; (8) have osteoporosis; (9) are elderly; (10) have lost their sense of smell or taste; (11) possess a birthmark; (12) have acne scars.

2. Claim all of the above "disabilities" that you have. Describe how your disability(s) negatively affect your capacity to fully participate in parish life. Then answer this question: Is it right to expect that someone with one or more of the three major disabilities should find participation in parish life any less fulfilling than you do?

CHAPTER ELEVEN

Other Concerns

And the Stories Go On

Let the little children come to me....
MARK 10:14

U nexpected dimensions about disabilities were offered to the participants by two other women: one woman whose story significantly affected the workshop participants was the mother of an emotionally disturbed son. Her story brings to mind the words of Jesus:

> *People were bringing children to him [Jesus] in order that he might touch them; and the disciples spoke sternly to them. But when Jesus saw this, he was indignant and said to them, "Let the little children come to me; do not stop them; for it is to such as these that the kingdom of God belongs. Truly I tell you, whoever does not receive the kingdom of God as a little child will never enter it." And he took them up in his arms, laid his hands on them, and blessed them.*
> MARK 10:13–16

The mother was eager to tell about how successfully her local parish responded to her son's sometimes erratic behavior. Frequently, he joined in receiving the body and blood of Christ with the entire community. They were used to him and had no problem with that. But one morning a visiting priest, unfamiliar with the parish's custom,

81

was startled when the little boy, receiving a wafer instead of the familiar piece of bread, simply spat it out of his mouth. A regular parish priest who knew the boy, retrieved the sacred species and pocketed it for later respectful disposal.

Mothers in the group smiled at this anecdote, and it lightened the seriousness of our discussion. We could appreciate the compassion of the priest's quick response and wondered what we might have done. Laughter tended to relax the group and brought in the human value behind what we were discussing.

In *A Rumor of Angels: Modern Society and the Rediscovery of the Supernatural* (New York: Anchor Books, 1970), author Peter Berger comments as follows:

> *This is the comic relief of redemption, it makes it possible for us to laugh and to play with a new fullness. This in no way implies a remoteness from the moral challenges of the moment, but rather the most careful attention to each human gesture that we encounter or that we may be called upon to perform in the everyday dramas of human life—literally, an "infinite care" in the affairs of men—just because, in the words of the New Testament writer, it is in the midst of these affairs that "some have entertained angels unawares" (Heb 13:2).*

In the depths of such reflections, participants began to realize the overwhelming power of laughter that occurs when disabilities are put into proper perspective. One participant recognized that while laughing at their stories she felt no pity for our speakers, all of whom have major disabilities. "I used to pray for each person with a disability in my ministry—that God's grace would heal them and make them whole. I do not indulge in that type of self-righteous request any longer. Instead, I thank God for the chance of seeing beyond the disabilities to the possibilities of grace and grandeur of spirit that might well take root and grow in their souls—and mine as well.

Another mother whose nine-year-old son, Tyler, has taught her the meaning of being rich in spirit explains. This recounting is taken from *Just As I Am: Americans With Disabilities* (Birmingham: Crane Hill, 1999).

> *Tyler was born with severe autism, which can cause mental retardation, language and speech deficits, and behavioral problems. There is no cure.*
>
> *Tyler's mother says, "I've always wanted to be a good mother. More than anything else, Tyler has changed my concept of what that is. I've had this fantasy of seeing my children at their college graduation. After the ceremony, all the family goes to a nice restaurant to celebrate the occasion. I've realize that not only will Tyler never go to college, he won't even be able to sit at the restaurant with us....I want Tyler to have an enviable life, which is a life of people loving you and you loving them. That's what makes us rich.*

The Wounded Healer

The second participant who had a profound effect on the workshop participants was a newly ordained pastor. I had met Jeannie at a Pathways Awareness Foundation meeting where she was seated next to me in her wheelchair. When she joined us for a workshop at CTU, she surprised me as she rose from her wheelchair and walked to the podium. Jeannie is pastor at a suburban Lutheran church. She told us much about her life and work as a pastor. She had been called to her first parish almost immediately after ordination. However, before long she was stricken with a latent disease that weakened her muscles so severely that she had to use a wheelchair in order to continue her work. Responding to the crisis, her congregation made the altar accessible with modifications for her wheelchair.

She also spoke of the life-giving information she had received through the Pathways Awareness Foundation, which has enabled her to regain limited mobility. The foundation was established in 1987, and countless families have depended on it for support, information, programs, and news of medical advancements for early intervention.

The Pathways early intervention program can result in a diagnosis and appropriate treatment program to greatly reduce more serious effects of neurological problems. Simply by learning the proper treatment and medication that can inhibit and even mitigate adverse conditions, some people have been led to permanent stability in later life. Through research, Jeanie discovered that her own daughter will suffer the same disability she has. If not detected at an early stage, her daughter will endure the same muscular problems Jeannie experiences. Through early intervention, Pathways has enabled Jeannie to prevent the advancement of her daughter's disease, as it has done for countless other children as well.

Pathways sponsored Cardinal Bernardin's convocation, *That All May Worship*, in 1996. During the convocation, Father Henry Nouwen spoke of his work at *L'Arche*, a community for individuals who are mentally challenged. Childlike in their innocence and simple in their acts of love and gratitude, these people reinvigorated this holy man. He shared the following story during the convocation.

Once at Mass, a newly widowed woman who was still grieving, began weeping inconsolably. Her distressing sobs caused the priest to stop, perplexed, not sure how to help. Finally, a resident of *L'Arche* crossed over to her side and put his arm around her shoulder. Leaning on him, she quickly calmed down and the weeping softened so the liturgy could continue. It was such a simple act; a gentle gesture by one whose own simplicity restored peace and gave comfort to someone in deep sorrow.

Questions for
Reflection and Discussion

1. Recall and share an experience you have been present for when humor helped relieve a tense situation involving someone in an everyday circumstance or someone who was disabled.
2. Evaluate this comment:

The problem with people like the severely disabled matinee idol who puts his celebrity in the service of cure rather than care is that he is not only highly visible but that he unfortunately echoes the wild expectations of the population. It's troubling because this attitude seems to dominate public discourse about what the response to the disability is.

Challenge

1. Ask a person whose life has been drastically changed by an accident or a debilitating illness about the adaptations they had to make to adjust to the life changes forced upon them.

2. Imagine living in a community, like *L'Arche*, where the majority of residents have severe disabilities and only the minority are not disabled. Circle the words below that for you would best describe that living situation and share with others why you chose those words.

depressing	loving	lonely
happy	limiting	challenging
tiresome	fulfilling	pitiful

3. Apply the following quote from Nelson Mandela to the efforts of people with disabilities to be included in the events of ordinary life:

   We ask ourselves, who am I to be brilliant, gorgeous, talented, fabulous? Actually, who are you not to be? You are a child of God. Your playing small does not serve the world....We were born to make manifest the glory of God that is within us. It is not just in some of us; it is in everyone."

4. In the following paragraphs, ethicist Adrienne Asch recounts her thoughts on passing on her disability of retinitis pigmentosa and blindness to her children. How would you deal with the thought of passing on a genetically based disability, for example, Huntington's chorea, to your children?

Though I find the view that only the healthy should be allowed to live appalling, I have never had to attend to anything more serious than the question of continuing the genetic line of retinitis pigmentosa and thus blindness. When I recently said those words to a friend, his momentary silence communicated his shock. "More serious than blindness?" he finally said. "What could be more serious than blindness?"

Though I realize that for most people, the possibility of genetically transmitting blindness is hardly appealing, my children's view of this would be shocking to the members of that chorus. They are not only glad to be alive in spite of my daughter's having inherited retinitis pigmentosa from me, they are also, to my surprise, not particularly concerned with the possibility of saddling their own children with it. "If I have to have a kid with RP, I'll take it," my daughter said.

CHAPTER TWELVE

Why Did He Choose Me?

The God of Disabilities

Out of the depths I cry to you, O LORD!
Lord, hear my voice!

PSALM 130:1

"It's just a wheelchair," said seven-year-old Taria Jackson, to the woman who was staring at her in Wal-Mart. "I just can't walk. I'm not any different from anyone else. God made us all in His image, so at some time God was in a wheelchair."

JUST AS I AM: AMERICANS WITH DISABILITIES.
PHOTOGRAPHS BY CAROLYN SHERER AND TEXT BY ELLEN DOSSETT,
BIRMINGHAM, ALABAMA: CRANE HILL, 1999.

Just as Job had difficulty in understanding how God could have given him so many severe losses to bear, we too sometimes wonder how God could give so many people disabilities that seem almost insurmountable. The secret is faith in the God who gives no one more than he or she can bear. The Old Testament story that follows shows the hope of those whose faith in God is unshakable.

Shadrach, Meshach, and Abednego answered the king, "O Nebuchadnezzar, we have no need to present a defense to you in this matter. If our God whom we serve is able to deliver us from the furnace of blazing fire and out of your hand, O king,

let him deliver us! But if not, be it known to you, O king, that
we will not serve your gods and we will not worship the golden
statue that you have set up" (Dan 3:16–18).

What kind of a God would allow three young men with such strong faith to be cast into a fiery furnace? What kind of a God would ask Abraham to sacrifice his only son, Isaac, and then at the last moment provide him with an animal for the slaughter? What kind of a God would not heed the cry of his own son, sweating blood in the garden at Gethsemane? How could God hear the prayer, "Abba, Father,…remove this cup from me…" (Mk 14:36), and turn away his face?

People with various disabilities struggle with the temptation of miraculous cures and release from whatever torment they endure. Sometimes miracles do happen—medications are manufactured and operations are perfected so that the lame walk, the blind see, and the deaf receive the latest implant. All these are modern miracles. And there were ancient ones, too. I believe miracles do occur. O God, "if you choose" to perform a miracle for us, we thank you with humility and joy.

However, the God who lavishes grace upon us, who gave the gift of faith to our father, Abraham, who seemed to deny his own beloved Son in the garden, and who sent angels to the three young men as they strolled amid the flames in the red hot furnace—that is the God I believe in and worship.

That God is not manipulated by my desires, but offers me grace to carry on in the midst of pain and doubt. That God is not a pushover, but stands alongside me as I ask to accept the grace at hand. That God sees my humiliation when I am denied a job because of my disability. That God also breathes the spirit of determination in me to see justice done when I am denied work for which I am qualified.

That God loves with the toughness of grace and the comfort of support when all seems lost. That God says, "My yoke is easy and my burden is light" (Mt 11:30), and invites me to come and follow. The

God of the disabled offers grace to accept and then to rejoice with the ecstasy that comes with acceptance.

Saint Paul knew that as he pleaded to have the thorn in his flesh removed. He also understood as he accepted the grace that eased his pain and suffering. "Three times I appealed to the Lord about this, that it would leave me. But he said to me, 'My grace is sufficient for you, for power is made perfect in weakness'" (2 Cor 12:8–9). That God is for those who have matured through both suffering and blessings.

When Jesus appeared after the Resurrection, God did not erase the wounds in his hands and feet, or cover up the gash in his side. Instead, those things were glorified and are as much a part of the risen Christ as was his tender smile when Mary Magdalene embraced him in the garden. The God of the disabled is strong, firm, and constant, and the rewards of his love are deep, everlasting and rich with hope and compassion for all who suffer.

The three young men defied the king and faced the flames. They said to him, "We will not serve your gods" (Dan 3:18). But some do deny faith, loudly taunting individuals with disabilities, "If you really believed, you would be healed!" Well-meaning people approach individuals with disabilities to assure them that God can heal them. They even lay hands upon the unsuspecting victim. This type of situation occurs too often and probably can never be stopped.

Yet a word must be said for the God who does not seem to yield to the endless prayers, novenas, and petitions that rise on behalf of those who endure disabilities. God's response to all our prayers came when his Son took flesh upon himself and became obedient to death.

> *Who, though he was in the form of God,*
> *did not regard equality with God*
> *as something to be exploited,*
> *but…*
> *he humbled himself,*
> *and became obedient to the point of death—*
> *even death on a cross (Phil 2:6–8).*

And, I dare to add, he became our disabled God, leaving us an example *par excellence.*

The God of the disabled is a transcendent God, pointing us toward signposts of his presence in our midst. If we can see them, they will take us past the here and now to a beauty that lies beyond our disabilities and even beyond the crucifixion. As Dietrich Bonhoeffer wrote, "All historical events are 'penultimate,' in that their ultimate significance lies in a reality that transcends them..." (cited in *A Rumor of Angels*, Peter Berger, New York: Anchor Books, 1970).

Questions for Reflection and Discussion

1. What miracles have you witnessed in the world?
2. Discuss among your group what is the best way to answer someone who complains that God does not hear or does not answer their prayers.
3. In the light of this chapter, how would you explain the attraction of Lourdes for those who are disabled?

Challenge

1. Ask a person with a major disability what it is they need most in their life. Does their answer surprise you?

CHAPTER THIRTEEN

A Summing Up

Where Do We Go From Here?

A person who is severely impaired never knows his hidden sources of strength until he is treated like a normal human being and encouraged to shape his own life.

HELEN KELLER

D espite all the good intentions and positive suggestions for inclusion in our lives and in our parishes, we must return once more to the underlying fear all of us face. People with disabilities of any sort pose an unspoken threat to others because often what we avoid confronting is what inwardly we dread most. We also are fearful of our inability to face up to the challenges that are faced by people who have disabilities.

The near presence of someone in a wheelchair, or laboring with any disability, may cause feelings of anxiety. (What other challenge might God ask me to accept?) I understand that, even though I have lived with blindness for many years. The possibility of further limitations poses an awesome dread. I don't want to even think about such an unpleasant potential. Thus, I tried to rationalize my feelings about not visiting my poor mother-in-law while she was enduring cancer therapy, claiming that I simply couldn't face visiting her in the hospital. "Wait till she comes home," was my mantra. Some inner fear warded me off. It was the "I might catch something" syndrome.

We all have fears, and perhaps the best way to confront fear is to bring it into open discussion. I believe honest, open discussion of this very difficult subject is vitally necessary if we are ever going to get beyond fear into real inclusion.

Once, on a day set aside to help persons training for ministry understand people laboring with physical impairments, participants were instructed ahead of time to select and enact a disability. Some arrived at class with crutches, some wheeling themselves about, clumsily, down corridors and through doors too narrow for cumbersome wheelchairs.

Some of the more adventurous students blindfolded themselves and, with sighted partners, went out onto the public street to make their way around. One approached a fellow student with her guide-dog and asked if he might hold onto her arm and go for a faith walk with his eyes blindfolded. "Really cool!" some said as he walked by cautiously.

The day ended with everyone returning to their normal physical situation and the discussion began in earnest. For most it was fun for a while, but all were relieved to step back into their familiar physical reality at the end of the experiment. (They also acknowledged that the realization that they could do so at any time helped to sustain them through the ordeal.)

I couldn't help but reflect on what happens in schools where guide-dogs are trained. When the dog has completed the training, its trainer, blindfolded, takes the animal in harness out into the city streets. The purpose of the exercise is to evaluate the dog's performance in crossing streets, boarding busses, and going into a store to shop. It also shows the trainer's confidence in the dog, a result of his own training skills.

I once overheard a trainer speaking in low serious tones to his newly trained dog, "You better not make me stumble over a curb or bump into a door, or else we're going to have a serious talk when we get back." I wondered if that was wishful thinking, but it also contains a bit of wisdom: simply donning a blindfold or hobbling about on a pair of crutches does not really afford a true experience of disability.

Like the dog trainer, participants in these exercises can always look forward to "when we get back."

Each disability calls for learning a very specific and demanding set of skills. A person must learn and use those alternate skills if he or she is to become sufficiently competent to engage in a job, a journey, or in life. And life does exist, richly and rewardingly, even after a disability.

A final example might help: Once, teaching my usual college-level course in English composition to a group of freshmen, I was surprised when one young medical student came to speak to me. He told me that he had gone to his room, blindfolded himself and began to grope about to find this or that. He said, "I couldn't find anything at all! You are simply amazing!" He could not understand how I did anything.

So I said, "George, go back to your room. When you get there, do not put on the blindfold again; get on your computer and get the paper finished that is due tomorrow morning. Exercise your student skills, and never mind the blindness skills. You would learn them if had to."

And so he did.

Questions for Reflection and Discussion

1. What fears do you have about growing old and becoming less able to function physically, especially if degenerative disease in present in your family history?
2. What measures could you take now to prepare for that eventuality in life? Could those same measures be applied in your parish setting to aid folks who have those disabilities now?

Challenges

1. Imagine that you will have to acquire some disability as the result of an accident or debilitating disease. What disability do you think would be the most difficult to adjust to and why?
2. Talk to some with the disability you considered in number 1 above, and ask them what is most difficult in life for them…and what is their greatest blessing.
3. Whether you are currently disabled or fully able-bodied, give thanks to God for the gift and blessing of life.

Demographics of Disability

The following statistics on Catholics with disabilities in the United States were prepared by the National Catholic Partnership on Disability based on a National Organization on Disability/Harris Survey of Americans With Disabilities performed in 2000. We are grateful to the NCPD and its director, Mary Jane Owen, for permission to reprint excerpts.

Total Number of Catholics Defined As Disabled

- 14 million Catholics in the U.S. can be defined as disabled.
- Approximately 6 million U.S. Catholics have more than one disability.
- 280,000 American Catholics live with *severe* disabilities.

Types of Disabling Conditions

- 8.1 million American Catholics have a physical disability. (These include orthopedic impairments, neuromuscular or muscular disabilities, and brain dysfunction.)
- 1.3 million U.S. Catholics have sensory disabilities.
- Approximately 560,000 Catholics are blind or visually impaired.
- Nearly the same number are deaf or hard of hearing.
- 560,000 Catholics in America are mentally retarded or cognitively disabled.
- 16,800 can classified as severely mentally retarded.
- 700,000 Catholics are classified as mentally ill.
- 24 percent of those with disabilities, or about 3.6 million Catholics, have assorted health problems that limit daily living functions.

Age at Which Disabilities Among Catholics Tend to Develop

- 13 percent of disabled people became disabled somewhere from birth through adolescence. These are called "developmental disabilities" since they occurred during the person's developmental years.

- 21 percent of disabled people became disabled as young adults.
- 22 percent of disabled people became disabled during their middle years.
- 37 percent (the largest group) of those who are disabled became so after age fifty-five.

Employment Status of Americans with Disabilities

- Only three in ten people with disabilities of working age are employed full or part time, compared to eight in ten for persons without disabilities.
- Two out of three unemployed people with disabilities would prefer to be working.

Attendance at Religious Services

- Only half the percentage of adults with disabilities attend church services compared to those without disabilities.

Parish
Self-Assessment Tool

Access: It Begins in the Heart

How well are you doing? For each of the fifteen levels in the journey of your congregation, select the bubble that best matches current progress. You will notice that each level of the journey represents a greater commitment on the part of the congregation toward
the goal of full participation of people with disabilities.

The National Organization on Disability, Religion and Disability Program, 910
16th St. NW., Washington, DC 20006.

	THE JOURNEY OF A CONGREGATION	Not started	Getting started	Well on our way	We're there
1	AWARENESS: Recognition by some congregation members or the ordained religious leadership that certain barriers were preventing children or adults with physical, sensory, or mental disabilities from accessing a full life of faith (including worship, study, service, and leadership).	◯	◯	◯	◯
2	ADVOCACY (Internal): Growing advocacy within the congregation to welcome people with disabilities as full participants and to remove barriers (architectural, communications, and attitudes) to this participation.	◯	◯	◯	◯
3	DISCUSSIONS: Concerns raised regarding ability of the congregation to meet the challenges (for example: Are there enough people with this need to justify the expense? Will people with disabilities feel comfortable in joining us once barriers have been removed?) and then solutions identified—ideally with input from people with disabilities and other experts.	◯	◯	◯	◯
4	PLANS: Invitation of people with disabilities to join the congregation as full members (including participation in rites of passage and initiation), action plans devised to achieve barrier-removing goals, and formal commitment made to welcome people with disabilities.	◯	◯	◯	◯

5	ACCOMMODATIONS: Accommodations made to improve the participation of people with disabilities (for example, large-print bulletins, trained ushers, accessible parking spaces, ramps and pew cuts, improved lighting and sound systems, appropriate religious education for children with disabilities).	◯	◯	◯	◯
6	WELCOMING ENVIRONMENT: Appreciation expressed for the changes being made and friendships extended to people with disabilities and their family members by increasing numbers within the congregation.	◯	◯	◯	◯
7	HURDLES: Identification of architectural (for example, elevator, accessible rest room, ramp to the altar, chancel, or bimah), communications (for example, sign-language interpreter or alternative formats for materials), transportation (for example, wheelchair accessible van), financial, or other barriers and ways found to move forward in spite of them.	◯	◯	◯	◯
8	INCLUSION: Increased participation of people with disabilities in worship, study, and service to others, as well as increased comfort levels of members with a more diverse congregation.	◯	◯	◯	◯
9	OUTREACH (Local): Options explored and action plans formulated for partnership opportunities with local agencies and organizations serving people with disabilities.	◯	◯	◯	◯

	THE JOURNEY OF A CONGREGATION	Not started	Getting started	Well on our way	We're there
10	LEADERSHIP: Recruitment of lay members with disabilities for leadership roles within the congregation and a willingness demonstrated to accept and accommodate an ordained leader with disability.	○	○	○	○
11	NEW CONSCIOUSNESS: Resistant barriers of attitude within the congregation toward people with disabilities addressed (for example, through adult-education forums, interactive experiences for children, consciousness raising by the leadership of the congregation, and one-on-one friendships).	○	○	○	○
12	TRANSFORMATION: Ongoing transformation of the congregation (through enriched opportunities, responsibilities, and friendships) into a place where children and adults with disabilities are welcomed, fully included, and treated with respect.	○	○	○	○
13	ADVOCACY (External): An expanded advocacy role for congregation members regarding the needs and rights of persons with disabilities in the community at large.	○	○	○	○
14	OUTREACH: Successful strategies, insights, and effective practices compiled and shared with other congregations and communities.	○	○	○	○
15	SHARING THE STORY: The story of the transformation of the congregation publicized through articles, presentations, and/or media events.	○	○	○	○

APPENDIX C

Resources

Organizations and Web Sites

National Catholic Partnership on Disability advances inclusion in Church: 415 Michigan Avenue, NE, Suite 240, Washington, DC 20017-4501; (202) 529-2933 / TTY (202) 529-2934; www.ncpd.org.

National Apostolate for Inclusion Ministry supports the inclusion of persons with mental retardation and developmental disabilities in the Catholic Church: P.O. Box 218, Riverdale, MD 20738; (800) 736-1280; www.nafim.org /resources.html.

National Catholic Office for the Deaf, 7202 Buchanan Street, Lanover Hills, MD 20784-2236; voice (301) 577-1684; TTY (301) 577-4184; www.ncod.org.

SPRED: Special Religious Development is a network of services in the archdiocese of Chicago, designed to assist persons with developmental disabilities and/or learning problems to become integrated into parish assemblies of worship through the process of education in their faith. It can be reached at the following address: Archdiocese of Chicago, 2956 South Lowe Avenue, Chicago, IL 60616; (312) 842-1039; www.spred.org.

Faith & Light is a spiritual movement supporting persons with developmental disabilities, their families and friends. One of their goals is to integrate its members in the churches: (508) 349-2514; www.faithandlight.net.

Family Village Worship Center provides religious/faith/spiritual resources for those who have disabilities: www.familyvillage.wisc.edu/worship.htm.

National Council of Churches Committee on Disabilities seeks wholeness in Christ's church by promoting the full inclusion and participation of all persons: c/o Ministries in Christian Education, National Council of Churches of Christ, 475 Riverside Drive, Room 848, New York, NY 10115; www.ncccusa.org/nmu /mce/dis/.

Network of Inclusive Catholic Educators is made up of administrators, educators, and parents creating opportunities for children with disabilities to attend Catholic schools and religious-education programs. Contact at the following: Institute for Pastoral Initiatives, University of Dayton, Dayton, OH 45469-0314; 1 (888) 532-3389; www.udayton.edu/~ipi/nice/index.php3.

Special Needs Resource Directory for Catholic Schools and Religious Education Programs can be accessed at www.usccb.org/education/fedasst/needs4.pdf.

National Information Center for Children and Youth With Disabilities shares information about disabilities in children and youth. It is located at: P.O. Box 1492; Washington, DC 20013; (800) 695-0285; www.nichcy.org.

Parent Advocacy in Special Education: Strategies, Supports and Quality Control is an on-line course for parents, empowering them to effectively advocate for their children with disabilities. Cost $25.00. http://home.universalclass.com/I /crn/2108.htm.

Pathways Awareness Foundation seeks to increase public and professional awareness about early detection, early prevention and inclusion of children and youth with physical challenges. It is located at: 150 North Michigan Avenue, Suite 2100, Chicago, IL 60601; www.pathwaysawareness.org.

The Fathers Network celebrates and supports fathers and families raising children with special healthcare needs and developmental disabilities. It can be reached at: 16120 - NE 8th Street, Bellevue, WA 98008-3937; www.fathersnetwork.org.

The Family Village is a global community of disability related resources. It can be accessed at the following address: Waisman Center, University of Wisconsin-Madison, 1500 Highland Avenue, Madison, WI 53705-2280; www.familyvillage .wisc.edu/index.htmlx.

Developmental Disabilities Leadership Forum offers courses, discussion groups, articles, and conferences/events to anyone interested in developmental disability; www.ddleadership.org.

Access Living fosters the dignity, pride, and self-esteem of people with disabilities and enhances their options so they may maintain individualized and satisfying lifestyles. It may be reached at the following: 614 West Roosevelt Road, Chicago, IL 60607; (312) 253-7000, (312) 253-7002 TTY; www.accessliving.org.

The Arc of the United States works to include all children and adults with cognitive, intellectual and developmental disabilities in every community. (301) 565-3842; www.thearc.org.

The Progress Center is a community-based, nonprofit, nonresidential, service and advocacy organization, operated for people with disabilities by people with disabilities. It is located at: 7521 Madison Street; Forest Park, IL 60130; (708) 209-1500, TTY (708) 209-1826; http://progresscil.org.

National Organization on Disability provides opportunities to increase participation of people with disabilities in communities and in religious participation. Also has a checklist for determining the accessibility of your parish community. It may be reached at: 910 Sixteenth Street NW, Suite 600; Washington, DC 20006; (202) 293-5960, TTY (202) 293-5968; www.nod.org.

National Federation of the Blind helps blind persons achieve self-confidence and self-respect and to act as a vehicle for collective self-expression by the blind: 1800 Johnson Street, Baltimore, MD 21230; (410) 659-9314; www.nfb.org.

Blind Net is a listing of organizations and services for the blind: www.blind.net.

American Association of Persons with Disabilities is dedicated to ensuring economic self-sufficiency and political empowerment for the more than 56 million Americans with disabilities. AAPD works in coalition with other disability organizations for the full implementation and enforcement of disability nondiscrimination laws. It is located at: 1629 K Street NW, Suite 503; Washington, DC 20006; (202) 457-0046 V/TTY 800-840-8844; www.aapd.com.

The Council for Disability Rights advances the rights and enhances the lives of people with disabilities. Its offices are at: 205 West Randolph, Suite 1645; Chicago, IL 60606; (312) 444-9484, TDD (312) 444-1967; www.disability rights.org.

National Council on Disability promotes policies, programs, practices, and procedures that guarantee equal opportunity for all individuals with disabilities, and to empower individuals with disabilities to achieve economic self-sufficiency, independent living, and inclusion and integration into all aspects of society: 1331 F Street, NW, Suite 850; Washington, DC 20004; voice: (202) 272-2004, TTY: (202) 272-2074; www.ncd.gov/index.html.

Paralyzed Veterans of America is a service organization with expertise on the needs of veterans of the armed forces with spinal cord injury or dysfunction: 801 Eighteenth Street, NW; Washington, DC 20006-3517; 1 (800) 424-8200; www.pva.org.

The World Institute on Disability is a nonprofit research, training and public policy center promoting civil rights and full societal inclusion of people with disabilities: 510 16th Street, Suite 100, Oakland, CA 94612; voice: (510) 763-4100; TTY: (510) 208-9496; www.wid.org.

Links to Other Disability Resources: http://soeweb.syr.edu/thechp/disres.htm.

Religion and Disability: www.disabilityresources.org/RELIGION.html.

Human Disability and the Service of God provides a selected bibliography on disability and religion: www.pitts.emory.edu/exchange/history/HTML/disabilities/bibliography.html.

Center for the Study of Religion and Disability: www.geocities.com/Athens/2926/.

Disability Concerns offers annotated bibliographies on the following topics: (1) Developmental Disabilities and the Church, (2) Persons With Disabilities: Pastoral Care Resources, (3) Mental Illness and the Church, (4) Accessibility and Inclusion.

Checklist assessment form to determine how accessible your parish community is to the disabled: http://gbgm-umc.org/DISC/.

Available Resources in Print

Opening Doors to People with Disabilities
Volume I: Pastoral Manual (available on audio cassette)
215 page manual, provides specific information in a concise, easy-to-read for-
    mat. 1-9 copies: $12.00 each; 10 or more copies: $10.50 each.
Volume II: The Resource File (available on audio cassette)
1,400 page encyclopedia, neatly packaged in two loose-leaf binders to provide
    flexibility in research and in planning for workshops and conferences. 1-9
    sets: $55 each; 10 or more sets: $50 each.

A Loving Justice: The Moral and Legal Responsibilities of the U.S. Catholic Church
    under the Americans with Disabilities Act. A practical, 58-page user-friendly
    guide to the requirements for church entities of the landmark civil rights
    legislation for people with disabilities. (Available in audio cassette and large-
    type print.) 1-9 copies: $7.50 each; 10 or more copies: $6.50 each.

"Disability Ministry: Perspectives on Disability." A video to stimulate group
    discussion and awareness, featuring a series of vignettes which may be used
    separately if desired. Topics include: definition of disability; demographics
    of disability; perspective on the paralyzed man; theological implications of
    disability; the value of every life; and Blessed Margaret of Castello ($10 each).

The three previous titles are available through The National Catholic Partnership on Disability, 415 Michigan Avenue, NE, Suite 240, Washington, DC 20017-4501; (202) 529-2933; www.ncpd.org. Please note that shipping and handling are extra.

National Catholic Partnership on Disability serves as the national voice advocating for fulfillment of the challenges issued by the U.S. Conference of Catholic Bishops in their three documents calling for welcome and justice for people with the whole range of disabilities within the church and society. Through its resources, conferences, published articles and testimony, it illustrates the giftedness of every life working through a national network of diocesan level leaders charged by their bishops to oversee inclusion and welcome at the local level.

The Inclusion Awareness Day Workbook provides tools to welcome persons with disabilities every day of the year. It is available through Pathways Awareness Foundation, 150 North Michigan Avenue, Chicago, IL 60601; 1 (800) 955-2445.

Opening Hearts, Minds and Doors: Embodying the Inclusive and Vulnerable Love of God. Available for $3.00 through Pathways Awareness Foundation, 150 North Michigan Avenue, Chicago, IL 60601; 1 (800) 955-2445; www.pathways awareness.org; or write to The National Federation of Priest Councils, 1337 West Ohio Street, Chicago, IL 60622.

Xavier Society provides free Braille and large-print missals and bibles. It is located at 154 E. 23rd Street, New York, NY 10010; 1 (800) 637-9193 or (212) 473-7800.

Developmental Disabilities and Sacramental Access: New Paradigms for Sacramental Encounters. Written by theologians and experts in special education, this book demonstrates how people with developmental disabilities need to be embraced by the Church and its sacraments, for they teach us something central about sacramental encounters. Edited by Edward Foley; $11.95; Collegeville, Minnesota: The Liturgical Press, 1994.

Brain Injury: When the Call Comes: A Congregational Resource. A resource booklet of information, strategies, personal stories, faith journeys, and resources for congregations, with a focus on New Jersey. Edited by The Brain Injury Association of New Jersey and The Boggs Center, 2001, 28 pages. Cost: $5.00 for out-of-state orders. Free to people in New Jersey. Brain Injury Association of New Jersey, Inc., 1090 King George Post Road, Suite 708, Edison, NJ 08837.

On the Road to Congregational Inclusion: Dimensions of Faith and Congregational Ministries With Persons With Developmental Disabilities and Their Families, 170 pages, 2002. Cost: $15. This book is a bibliography and address listing of resources for clergy, laypersons, families, and service providers. A resource guide divided into areas of congregational ministry and outreach; for example, worship, outreach, pastoral care, religious education, awareness videos, with sections on respite care, community building, person-centered planning, coping with grief, and more.

Garlic Press provides affordable Sign Language books and flash cards for church and classroom. It is located at 1312 Jeppesen Avenue, Eugene, OR 97401; (541) 345-0063; fax (541) 683-8767; http://www.garlicpress.com/.

U.S. Bishops Statements on Persons With Disabilites

U. S. Bishops Pastoral Statement on Welcome and Justice for Persons With Disabilities: A Framework of Access and Inclusion

Twenty years ago we issued a statement calling for inclusion of persons with disabilities in the life of the Church and community. In 1982 the National Catholic Office for Persons With Disabilities was established to promote this ministry. And in 1995 we strengthened our commitment with passage of the *Guidelines for the Celebration of the Sacraments With Persons With Disabilities.*

This moral framework is based upon Catholic documents and serves as a guide for contemplation and action. We hope that the reaffirmation of the following principles will assist the faithful in bringing the principles of justice and inclusion to the many new and evolving challenges confronted by persons with disabilities today.

1. We are a single flock under the care of a single shepherd. There can be no separate Church for people with disabilities.

2. Each person is created in God's image, yet there are variations in individual abilities. Positive recognition of these differences discourages discrimination and enhances the unity of the Body of Christ.

3. Our defense of life and rejection of the culture of death requires that we acknowledge the dignity and positive contributions of our brothers and sisters with disabilities. We unequivocally oppose negative attitudes toward disability which often lead to abortion, medical rationing, and euthanasia.

4. Defense of the right to life implies the defense of all other rights which enable the individual with the disability to achieve the fullest measure of personal development of which he or she is capable. These include the right to

equal opportunity in education, in employment, in housing, and in healthcare, as well as the right to free access to public accommodations, facilities, and services.

5. Parish liturgical celebrations and catechetical programs should be accessible to persons with disabilities and open to their full, active, and conscious participation, according to their capacity.

6. Since the parish is the door to participation in the Christian experience, it is the responsibility of both pastors and laity to assure that those doors are always open. Costs must never be the controlling consideration limiting the welcome offered to those among us with disabilities, since provision of access to religious functions is a pastoral duty.

7. We must recognize and appreciate the contribution persons with disabilities can make to the Church's spiritual life, and encourage them to do the Lord's work in the world according to their God-given talents and capacity.

8. We welcome qualified individuals with disabilities to ordination, to consecrated life, and to full-time, professional service in the Church.

9. Often families are not prepared for the birth of a child with a disability or the development of impairments. Our pastoral response is to become informed about disabilities and to offer ongoing support to the family and welcome to the child.

10. Evangelization efforts are most effective when promoted by diocesan staff and parish committees which include persons with disabilities. Where no such evangelization efforts exist, we urge that they be developed.

We join the Holy Father in calling for actions which "ensure that the power of salvation may be shared by all" (John Paul II, *Tertio Millennio Adveniente*, no. 19). Furthermore, we encourage all Catholics to study the original U.S. bishops and Vatican documents from which these principles were drawn.

Pastoral Statement of U.S. Catholic Bishops on People With Disabilities
November 16, 1978

1. The same Jesus who heard the cry for recognition from people with disabilities of Judea and Samaria 2,000 years ago calls us, his followers, to embrace our responsibility to our own disabled brothers and sisters in the United States. The Catholic Church pursues its mission by furthering the spiritual,

intellectual, moral, and physical development of the people it serves. As pastors of the Church in America, we are committed to working for a deeper understanding of both the pain and the potential of our neighbors who are blind, deaf, mentally retarded, emotionally impaired, who have special learning problems, or who suffer from single or multiple physical handicaps—all those whom disability may set apart. We call upon people of good will to reexamine their attitudes toward their brothers and sisters with disabilities and promote their well-being, acting with the sense of justice and the compassion that the Lord so clearly desires. Further, realizing the unique gifts handicapped individuals have to offer the church, we wish to address the need for their fuller integration into the Christian community and their fuller participation in its life.

2. Prejudice starts with the simple perception of difference, whether that difference is physical or psychological. Down through the ages, people have tended to interpret these differences in crude moral terms. *Our* group is not just different from *theirs*; it is better in some vague but compelling way. Few of us would admit to being prejudiced against people with disabilities. We bear them no ill will and do not knowingly seek to abrogate their rights. Yet people with disabilities are visibly, sometimes bluntly, different from the *norm*, and we react to this difference. Even if we do not look down upon handicapped people, we tend all too often to think of them as somehow apart—not fully *one of us.*

3. What individuals with disabilities need, first of all, is acceptance in this difference that can neither be denied nor overlooked. No act of charity or justice can be of lasting value unless our actions are informed by a sincere and understanding love that penetrates the wall of strangeness and affirms the common humanity underlying all distinction. Scripture teaches us that "any other commandment there may be [is] summed up in this: 'You shall love your neighbor as yourself' " (Rom 13:9). In his wisdom, Jesus said, "as yourself." We must love others from the inside out, so to speak, accepting their difference from us in the same way that we accept our difference from them.

4. Concern for people with disabilities was one of the prominent notes of Jesus' earthly ministry. When asked by John's disciples, "Are you he who is to come or are we to look for another?" Jesus responded with words recalling the prophecies of Isaiah. "Go back and report to John what you hear and see; the blind recover their sight, the lame walk, the lepers are cleansed, the deaf hear, dead men are raised to life, and the poor have the Gospel preached to them" (Mt 11:3–5). Persons with disabilities become witnesses for Christ, his healing of their bodies a sign of the spiritual healing he brought to all people. "Which

is less trouble to say, 'Your sins are forgiven' or 'Stand up and walk?'" To help you realize that the Son has authority on earth to forgive sins"—he then said to the paralyzed man—"Stand up! Roll up your mat and go home" (Mt 9:5f).

5. The Church that Jesus founded would surely have been derelict had it failed to respond to his example in its attention to people with disabilities. It remains faithful to its mission when its members become more and more a people of the Beatitudes, a people blessed in their meekness, their suffering, their thirst for righteousness. We all struggle with life. We must carry on this struggle in a spirit of mutual love, inspired by Christ's teaching that in serving others we serve the Lord himself (cf. Mt 25:40). In doing so, we build a community of interdependent people and discover the kingdom of God in our midst.

6. The Church, through the response of its members to the needs of others and through its parishes, healthcare institutions, and social service agencies, has always attempted to show a pastoral concern for individuals with disabilities. However, in a spirit of humble candor, we must acknowledge that at times we have responded to the needs of some of our people with disabilities only after circumstances or public opinion have compelled us to do so. By every means possible, therefore, the Church must continue to expand its healing ministry to these persons, helping them when necessary, working with them and raising its voice with them and with all members of society who are their advocates. Jesus revealed by his actions that service to and with people in need is a privilege and an opportunity as well as a duty. In extending our healing hands to others, we are healed ourselves.

7. On the most basic level, the Church responds to persons with disabilities by defending their rights. Pope John XXIII's encyclical *Pacem in Terris* stresses the innate dignity of all men and women. "In an ordered and productive community, it is a fundamental principle that every human being is a 'person'… [One] has rights and duties…flowing directly and spontaneously from [one's] very nature. These rights are therefore universal, inviolable, and inalienable" (no. 9).

8. The word *inalienable* reminds us that the principles on which our democracy is founded also guarantee certain rights to all Americans, regardless of their circumstances. The first of these, of course, is the right to life. We have spoken out on this issue on many occasions. We see defense of the right to life of persons with disabilities as a matter of particular urgency, however, because the presence of handicapping conditions is not infrequently used as a rationale for abortion. Moreover, those severely handicapped babies who are permitted to be born are sometimes denied ordinary and usual medical procedures.

9. All too often, abortion and postnatal neglect are promoted by arguing that the handicapped infant will survive only to suffer a life of pain and deprivation. We find this reasoning appalling. Society's frequent indifference to the plight of citizens with disabilities is a problem that cries aloud for solutions based on justice and conscience, not violence. All people have a clear duty to do what lies in their power to improve living conditions for people with disabilities, rather than ignoring them or attempting to eliminate them as a burden not worth dealing with.

10. Defense of the right to life, then, implies the defense of other rights which enable the individual with a disability to achieve the fullest measure of personal development of which he or she is capable. These include the right to equal opportunity in education, in employment, in housing, as well as the right to free access to public accommodations, facilities, and services. Those who must be institutionalized deserve decent, personalized care and human support as well as the pastoral services of the Christian community. Institutionalization will gradually become less necessary for some as the Christian community increases its awareness of disabled persons and builds a stronger and more integrated support system for them.

11. It is not enough merely to affirm the rights of people with disabilities. We must actively work to make them real in the fabric of modern society. Recognizing that individuals with disabilities have a claim to our respect because they are persons, because they share in the one redemption of Christ, and because they contribute to our society by their activity within it, the Church must become an advocate for and with them. It must work to increase the public's sensitivity toward the needs of people with disabilities and support their rightful demand for justice. Moreover, individuals and organizations at every level within the Church should minister to persons with disabilities by serving their personal and social needs. Many can function on their own as well as anyone in society. For others, aid would be welcome. All of us can visit persons unable to leave their homes, offer transportation to those who cannot drive, read to those who cannot read, speak out for those who have difficulty pleading their own case. In touching the lives of men, women and children in this way, we come closest to imitating Jesus' own example, which should be always before our eyes (cf. Lk 4:17, 19, 21).

12. Just as the Church must do all in its power to help ensure people with disabilities a secure place in the human community, so it must reach out to welcome gratefully those who seek to participate in the ecclesial community. The central meaning of Jesus' ministry is bound up with the fact that he sought

the company of people who, for one reason or another, were forced to live on the fringe of society (cf. Mk 7:37). These he made the special object of his attention, declaring that the last would be first and that the humble would be exalted in his Father's kingdom (cf. Mt 20:16, 23:12). The Church finds its true identity when it fully integrates itself with these *marginal* people, including those who suffer from physical and psychological disabilities.

13. If people with disabilities are to become equal partners in the Christian community, injustices must be eliminated and ignorance and apathy replaced by increased sensitivity and warm acceptance. The leaders and the general membership of the church must educate themselves to appreciate fully the contribution people with disabilities can make to the Church's spiritual life. Handicapped individuals bring with them a special insight into the meaning of life; for they live, more than the rest of us perhaps, in the shadow of the cross. And out of their experience they forge virtues like courage, patience, perseverance, compassion, and sensitivity that should serve as an inspiration to all Christians.

14. In the case of many people with disabilities, integration into the Christian community may require nothing more than issuing an invitation and pursuing it. For some others, however, full participation can only come about if the Church exerts itself to devise innovative programs and techniques. At the very least, we must undertake forms of evangelization that speak to the particular needs of individuals with disabilities, make those liturgical adaptations which promote their active participation, and provide helps and services that reflect our loving concern for those with serious problems.

15. This concern should be extended also to the families and especially the parents. No family is ever really prepared for the birth of a child with a disability. When such a child does come into the world, families often need strong support from their faith community. That support must remain firm with the passage of years. The path to independence for handicapped individuals can be difficult. Family members need to know that others stand with them, at least in spirit, as they help their children along this path.

16. The central importance of family members in the lives of all people with disabilities, regardless of age, must never be underestimated. They lovingly foster the spiritual, mental, and physical development of the disabled person and are the primary teachers of religion and morality. Ministers working in the apostolate with persons with disabilities should treat them as a uniquely valuable resource for understanding the various needs of those they serve.

17. Full participation in the Christian community has another important aspect that must not be overlooked. When we think of people with disabilities in relation to ministry, we tend automatically to think of doing something for them. We do not reflect that they can do something for us and with us. As noted above, people with disabilities can, by their example, teach the nondisabled person much about strength and Christian acceptance. Moreover, they have the same duty as all members of the community to do the Lord's work in the world, according to their God-given talents and capacity. Because handicapped individuals may not be fully aware of the contribution they can make, Church leaders should consult with them, offering suggestions on practical ways of serving.

18. For most Catholics the community of believers is embodied in the local parish. The parish is the door to participation for individuals with disabilities, and it is the responsibility of the pastor and lay leaders to make sure that this door is always open. We noted above that the task, on occasion, may not be an easy one; involving some people in parish life may challenge the ingenuity and commitment of the entire congregation. Yet, in order to be loyal to its calling, to be truly pastoral, the parish must make sure that it does not exclude any Catholic who wishes to take part in its activities.

19. If the participation of persons with disabilities and their families is to be real and meaningful, the parish must prepare itself to receive them. This preparation might begin with a census aimed at identifying parishioners and those with no church affiliation who have significant disabilities. Parish leaders could then work with individuals and their families to determine what steps, if any, are needed to facilitate their participation in parish life.

20. It may be necessary at this initial stage to place considerable emphasis upon educating the members of the parish community on the rights and needs of local people with disabilities. All too often, one hears that there are too few persons with disabilities in a given parish to warrant ramped entrances, special liturgies, or education programs. Some say that these matters should be handled on the diocesan level. Although many parishes have severely limited resources, we encourage all to make the best effort their circumstances permit. No parishioner should ever be excluded on the basis of disability alone.

21. The most obvious obstacle to participation in parish activities faced by many people with disabilities is the physical design of parish buildings. Structurally inaccessible buildings are at once a sign and a guarantee of their isolation from the community. Sometimes all that is required to remedy the situation is the installation of outside ramps and railings, increased lighting, minor modi-

fication of toilet facilities and, perhaps, the removal of a few pews and kneelers. In other cases, major alterations and redesign of equipment may be called for. Each parish must examine its own situation to determine the feasibility of such alterations. Mere cost must never be the exclusive consideration, however, since the provision of free access to religious functions for all interested people is a clear pastoral duty.

22. Whenever parishes contemplate new construction, they should make provision in their plans for the needs of individuals with disabilities. If both new construction and the adaptation of present buildings are out of the question, the parish should devise other ways to reach its members with disabilities. In cooperation with them, parish leaders may locate substitute facilities, for example, or make a concerted effort to serve at home those who cannot come to church.

23. It is essential that all forms of the liturgy be completely accessible to people with disabilities, since they are the essence of the spiritual tie that binds the Christian community together. To exclude members of the parish from these celebrations of the life of the Church, even by passive omission, is to deny the reality of that community. Accessibility involves far more than physical alterations to parish buildings. Realistic provision must be made for persons with disabilities to participate fully in the eucharist and other liturgical celebrations such as the sacraments of reconciliation, confirmation, and anointing of the sick. The experiences and needs of individuals with disabilities vary, as do those of any group of people. For some with significant disabilities, special liturgies may be appropriate. Others will not require such liturgies, but will benefit if certain equipment and services are made available to them. Celebrating liturgies simultaneously in sign language enables the deaf person to enter more deeply into their spirit and meaning. Participation aids such as Mass books and hymnals in large print or Braille serve the same purpose for blind or partially sighted members.

24. People can also play a more active role in the liturgy if provided with proper aids and training. Blind parishioners can serve as lectors, for example, and deaf parishioners as special ministers of the eucharist. In this connection, we look forward to the day when more handicapped individuals are active in the full-time, professional service of the Church, and we applaud recent decisions to accept qualified candidates for ordination or the religious life in spite of their significant disabilities.

25. Evangelization and catechesis for individuals with disabilities must be geared in content and method to their particular situation. Specialized catechists

should help them interpret the meaning of their lives and should give witness to Christ's presence in the local community in ways they can understand and appreciate. We hasten to add, however, that great care should be taken to avoid further isolation of people with disabilities through these programs which, as far as possible, should be integrated with the normal catechetical activities of the parish. We have provided guidelines for the instruction of persons with disabilities and for their participation in the liturgical life of the church in *Sharing the Light of Faith: National Catechetical Directory for Catholics of the United States.*

26. Finally, parishes must be sensitive to the social needs of members with disabilities. We have already touched on some ways in which Christians can express their concern for their brothers and sisters with disabilities. These actions and others like them can help solve some of the individual's practical problems and dispel a sense of isolation. They also create an opportunity for disabled and nondisabled people to join hands and break down the barriers that separate them. In such an interchange, it is often the person with a disability who gives the gift of most value.

27. Efforts to bring people with disabilities into the parish community are more likely to be effective if the parishes are supported by offices operating at the diocesan level. At present, the social-service needs of individuals with disabilities and their families are usually addressed by established diocesan agencies. Where it is found to be inadequate, the program should be strengthened to assure that specialized aid is provided to people with disabilities. In those cases where there is no program at all, we urge that one be established.

28. The clergy, religious, and laity engaged in this program should help the parish by developing policy and translating it into practical strategies for working with individuals with disabilities. They should serve as advocates, seeking help from other agencies. Finally, they should monitor public policy and generate multifaceted educational opportunities for those who minister to and with people with disabilities.

29. Many opportunities for action at the diocesan level now exist with regard to public policy. Three pieces of federal legislation that promise significant benefits to individuals with disabilities have been passed during the seventies; each calls for study and possible support. We refer to the Rehabilitation Amendments of 1974, and the Education for All Handicapped Children Act of 1975. Enforcement of the regulations implementing section 504 of the Rehabilitation Act, which forbids discrimination on the basis of disabling conditions, is a matter of particular interest. In response to the Rehabilitation Amendments,

the executive branch of the federal government has also taken recent action, sponsoring a White House Conference on Handicapped Individuals in 1977. This conference was attended by official state delegations, and there would be value in determining which of its recommendations are being applied in the state or states where a given diocese is located. Diocesan offices will also wish to keep abreast of general public policy and practice in their states.

30. Dioceses might make their most valuable contribution in the area of education. They should encourage and support training for all clergy, religious, seminarians and lay ministers, focusing special attention on those actually serving individuals with disabilities, whether in parishes or some other setting. Religious education personnel could profit from guidance in adapting their curricula to the needs of learners with disabilities, and Catholic elementary and secondary school teachers could be provided in-service training in how best to integrate students with disabilities into programs of regular education. The diocesan office might also offer institutes for diocesan administrators who direct programs with an impact on persons with disabilities.

31. The coordination of educational services within the dioceses should supplement the provision of direct educational aids. It is important to establish liaisons between facilities for people with disabilities operating under Catholic auspices (special, residential and day schools; psychological services and the like) and usual Catholic school programs. Only in this way can the structural basis be laid for the integration, where feasible, of students with disabilities into programs for the nondisabled persons. Moreover, in order to ensure handicapped individuals the widest possible range of educational opportunities, Catholic facilities should be encouraged to develop working relationships both among themselves and with private and public agencies serving the same population.

32. As the most visible expression of our commitment, we the bishops now designate ministry to people with disabilities as a special focus for the National Conference of Catholic Bishops and the U.S. Catholic Conference. This represents a mandate to each office and secretariat, as it develops its plans and programs, to address the concerns of individuals with disabilities. Appropriate offices should also serve as resource and referral centers to both parochial and diocesan bodies in matters relating to the needs of our brothers and sisters with disabilities.

33. People with disabilities are not looking for pity. They seek to serve the community and to enjoy their full baptismal rights as members of the Church. Our interaction with them can and should be an affirmation of our faith. There

can be no separate Church for people with disabilities. We are one flock that serves a single shepherd.

34. Our wholeness as individuals and as the people of God, we say again, lies in openness, service, and love. The bishops of the United States feel a concern for individuals with disabilities that goes beyond their spiritual welfare to encompass their total well-being. This concern should find expression at all levels. Parishes should maintain their own programs of ministry with people disabilities, and dioceses should make every effort to establish offices that coordinate this ministry and serve as resource and referral centers for parish efforts. Finally, the National Conference of Catholic Bishops and the U.S. Catholic Conference will be more vigilant in promoting ministry with persons with disabilities throughout the structure of the Church.

35. We look to the future with what we feel is a realistic optimism. The Church has a tradition of ministry to people with disabilities, and this tradition will fuel the stronger, more broadly based efforts called for by contemporary circumstances. We also have faith that our quest for justice, increasingly enlisted on the side of individuals with disabilities, will work powerfully in their behalf. No one would deny that every man, woman and child has the right to develop his or her potential to the fullest. With God's help and our own determination, the day will come when that right is realized in the lives of all people with disabilities.

Prayer for Those With Disabilities

O loving God, our Creator,
we pray for all who must live
day in and day out with disabilities.
We pray for those who have been permanently injured,
those who are frail from sickness
or wasted away in misery.
We pray for troubled children,
and for the dying.
May they all learn from the mystery
that the road of life and suffering takes them down,
on which Christ himself walked,
and which many of the saints have followed.
May their hearts trust you
even in pain and darkness.
We ask this in the name of Jesus,
who took all our infirmities upon himself.
Amen.